THE WEALTH FACTION FINANCIAL SERIES

THE VIABILITY OF ALTERNATIVE INVESTING

UNITY 1

Dedication:

This book is dedicated to my loving grandmother, Naomi Young Harris, whose presence in my life has been an immeasurable blessing. She has been my guiding light, my source of strength, and the foundation upon which my journey into the world of finance and education began.

In the early formative years of my life, it was my grandmother who took on the role of nurturing and raising me, instilling in me the values of hard work, resilience, and the importance of education. Alongside the support of many neighbors, family members, and unknown well-wishers who prayed and watched over me, she played a pivotal role in shaping the person I am today.

My grandmother, a powerful woman with an extraordinary ability to make things happen even in the face of limited financial resources, worked tirelessly as an Orderly and later as an Aid at the local hospital in Trenton, NJ. Her strength and determination taught me that success does not always come from wealth but from the unwavering spirit to persevere.

Through her, I learned about the challenges that Indigenous people, including the Black Foot Indian Tribe from her ancestral side, had endured for generations, especially during the 20th century. They faced immense difficulties due to the lack of access to money, credit, and other resources that were denied to them. Even those who managed to obtain valuable knowledge often faced three significant obstacles.

Firstly, some who gained knowledge chose not to share it with others, fearing that sharing the information would dilute their newfound status among their oppressors. Second, despite the knowledge being shared, many still lacked access to opportunities, perpetuating the cycle of inequality. And third, there were those resistant to change, unwilling to make sacrifices or embrace progress for the betterment of all. "Haters All Over!", as she would say. Accompanied by my grandmother, I recall visiting the bank on numerous occasions. She would share with me her earnings and the list of household bills, patiently explaining how money worked differently for women and men. She educated me on the importance of saving and enlightened me beyond the concept of a simple piggy bank.

Without her initial guidance and countless prayers, I would not have developed an interest in technology, education, mathematics, and so much more. She laid the foundation that has driven my passion for understanding and sharing knowledge.

Queen Naomi, I thank you from the depths of my heart for all you have done. This book is not only a tribute to you but also a testament to the sacrifices made by our ancestors, some even giving their lives, to provide people of color with the chance to succeed. As I pen these words, I pray that this book will not only make you proud but will also serve as a beacon of hope and empowerment for others, just as you have been for me. May it honor the legacy of resilience and determination that you bestowed upon me and inspire countless others to pursue their dreams and build a brighter future.

With utmost gratitude and love,

Steven L. Sykes (MR. LP)

CONTENTS

WHAT IS ALTERNATIVE INVESTING

Alternative investing refers to investment strategies and assets that fall outside the traditional realm of stocks, bonds, and cash. It encompasses a wide range of investment options that can include real estate, commodities, hedge funds, private equity, venture capital, cryptocurrencies, art, collectibles, and more. These investments often have different risk-return profiles, structures, and liquidity characteristics compared to traditional investments.

The primary goal of alternative investing is to diversify an investment portfolio beyond traditional asset classes. It allows investors to seek out unique opportunities, potentially generate higher returns, and mitigate risks by investing in assets that are not directly correlated to the broader financial markets. Alternative investments are typically less accessible to the general public and may require higher minimum investments or specialized knowledge.

Alternative investing can be appealing for several reasons. It offers the potential for higher returns due to the unique nature of the underlying assets or investment strategies. Additionally, alternative investments can provide diversification benefits by adding assets with low or negative correlations to traditional investments, which can help reduce portfolio volatility. Moreover, alternative investments can allow investors to participate in niche markets, support socially responsible initiatives, or capitalize on emerging trends or industries.

However, it's important to note that alternative investing often comes with higher risks and complexities. These investments may have limited liquidity, higher fees, regulatory considerations, and a longer time horizon for potential returns. Due diligence, thorough research, and understanding the associated risks are crucial before engaging in alternative investments. Consulting with financial professionals or advisors experienced in alternative investments is recommended to make informed decisions that align with individual investment objectives and risk tolerance.

THE BALANCE

We need to have a balanced life between those who have and those who have not.

1. Access to Non-Traditional Investments: Alternative investments provide opportunities beyond traditional stocks and bonds, which can be inaccessible or limited to certain groups. By offering avenues such as real estate investment trusts (REITs), peer-to-peer lending, and hedge funds, alternative investing allows a broader range of individuals to participate in potentially lucrative investments. This increased accessibility can help bridge the wealth gap by providing avenues for wealth accumulation and diversification to those who might not have had access before.

2. Entrepreneurship and Venture Capital: Alternative investing, particularly through venture capital, can support and fuel entrepreneurial endeavors. Startups and innovative businesses often rely on venture capital funding to grow and succeed. By investing in these early-stage companies, alternative investors can support entrepreneurs from underrepresented communities, including women, minorities, and individuals with limited access to traditional funding sources. This support can help create more equitable opportunities for wealth creation and narrow the wage gap.

3. Impact Investing and Social Enterprises: Impact investing focuses on generating positive social and environmental impact alongside financial returns. It involves directing capital towards companies, organizations, or projects that aim to address social and environmental challenges. Impact investments can contribute to reducing income inequality by supporting initiatives that target poverty alleviation, affordable housing, education, healthcare, and job creation. These investments not only generate returns but also have a direct positive impact on marginalized communities, thereby helping to narrow the wage gap.

4. Economic Development and Community Investments: Alternative investing can play a crucial role in community development and revitalization efforts. Investments in affordable housing projects, community infrastructure, small businesses, and microfinance initiatives can stimulate economic growth in underserved areas. By directing capital towards these community-based investments, alternative investors can create job opportunities, enhance local economies, and improve living standards. This, in turn, can contribute to reducing income disparities and improving wage levels within those communities.

5. Education and Financial Literacy: Alternative investing can also contribute to closing the wage gap by promoting education and financial literacy. By providing accessible platforms, resources, and educational materials about alternative investment opportunities, individuals from all backgrounds can gain knowledge and understanding about wealth creation and investment strategies. Improved financial literacy empowers individuals to make informed investment decisions,

increasing their chances of wealth accumulation and narrowing the wage gap.

6. Philanthropy and Impactful Giving: Alternative investors can also make a difference through strategic philanthropy. By combining their financial resources and expertise, they can support organizations and initiatives that focus on addressing income inequality, improving education, promoting job training, and enhancing access to healthcare and basic necessities. Philanthropic efforts can help uplift disadvantaged communities, creating more equitable opportunities and reducing the wage gap.

While alternative investing can contribute to equalizing the balance and improving the wage gap, it is important to acknowledge that it is part of a broader solution. Comprehensive efforts involving government policies, regulatory frameworks, equitable educational systems, inclusive social programs, and sustainable economic growth are needed to create lasting change and promote a more just and equitable society.

HOW ALTERNATIVE INVESTING CAN HELP THE BIPOC COMMUNITY CATCH UP?

Alternative investing has the potential to play a transformative role in helping the BIPOC (Black, Indigenous, and People of Color) community catch up and bridge existing wealth disparities. For far too long, systemic barriers and historical inequities have hindered wealth accumulation and access to traditional investment opportunities for marginalized communities. Alternative investing, with its diverse range of investment strategies and asset classes, offers an avenue for BIPOC individuals and communities to not only grow their wealth but also actively participate in sectors that have historically excluded them. By embracing alternative investments such as real estate, venture capital, impact investing, and small business funding, the BIPOC community can access pathways that have the potential to generate economic empowerment, foster entrepreneurship, and create positive social change. This article will explore the ways in which alternative investing can serve as a catalyst for financial inclusion and advancement, addressing the wealth gap and promoting economic equality for the BIPOC community.

1. Access to Capital: Alternative investing can help address the historical lack of access to capital faced by the BIPOC community.

Traditional financing channels have often been less accessible to BIPOC individuals and businesses due to systemic biases and discriminatory practices. Alternative investments, such as venture capital, private equity, or crowdfunding platforms, offer opportunities to secure funding for BIPOC entrepreneurs and startups. By providing access to capital, alternative investing can enable BIPOC-owned businesses to grow, create jobs, and generate wealth within their communities.

2. Minority-Owned Businesses: Alternative investing can specifically target and support minority-owned businesses, addressing the challenges they face in obtaining financing. Investments in BIPOC-owned businesses not only provide the necessary capital but also offer mentorship, guidance, and networking opportunities. This support helps build resilient businesses, fosters entrepreneurship within the BIPOC community, and contributes to economic empowerment and wealth creation.

3. Representation in Investment Management: Promoting diversity within alternative investment firms and fund management teams is crucial. Increasing representation of BIPOC professionals within these sectors ensures a broader range of perspectives and opportunities are considered in investment decisions. By actively seeking out and supporting BIPOC fund managers and investment professionals, alternative investing can contribute to more inclusive and equitable investment practices that benefit the BIPOC community.

4. Impact Investing: Impact investing can address social and environmental challenges that disproportionately affect the BIPOC

community. By directing investments towards businesses and projects that promote racial equity, affordable housing, education, healthcare, criminal justice reform, and community development, impact investing can generate positive change. These investments not only provide financial returns but also contribute to reducing systemic inequalities and creating more opportunities for the BIPOC community to thrive economically.

5. Education and Mentorship: Alternative investing can support educational initiatives and mentorship programs that equip the BIPOC community with the knowledge and skills needed to participate in wealth-building opportunities. By offering scholarships, training programs, and mentorship to BIPOC individuals interested in finance and alternative investments, the industry can help bridge the knowledge gap and promote inclusivity. Increased financial literacy and access to mentorship empower BIPOC individuals to navigate investment strategies effectively, make informed decisions, and capitalize on alternative investment opportunities.

6. Philanthropic Investments: Alternative investing can be utilized for philanthropic efforts targeting the BIPOC community. By strategically deploying capital towards organizations and projects focused on racial and economic inequalities, alternative investments can support initiatives such as affordable housing, community development, financial literacy programs, small business support, and workforce development. These investments contribute to long-term solutions, create economic opportunities, and foster greater financial equality within the BIPOC community.

7. Policy Advocacy and Systemic Change: Alternative investing can also play a role in advocating for policy changes that address systemic inequities and promote financial equality. By leveraging their influence and resources, alternative investors can support initiatives aimed at removing barriers, combating discrimination, and fostering an inclusive economic environment. This may include advocating for fair lending practices, promoting diversity and inclusion in corporate boardrooms, or supporting policy reforms that level the playing field for BIPOC entrepreneurs and investors.

8. Community Engagement and Collaboration: Alternative investors can actively engage with BIPOC communities to understand their specific needs and co-create solutions. By collaborating with local organizations, community leaders, and grassroots initiatives, alternative investors can ensure that their investments align with the priorities and aspirations of the communities they seek to support. This approach helps build trust, promote community ownership, and foster sustainable development.

It's important to note that while alternative investing can contribute to financial equality for the BIPOC community, it is part of a larger systemic change that requires collective efforts. Addressing historical inequities necessitates broader initiatives, including policy reforms, educational reforms, anti-discrimination measures, and inclusive economic development strategies. Collaboration among governments, corporations, financial institutions, community organizations, and individuals is essential for creating lasting change and promoting a more just and equitable society.

Real Estate Investment Trusts (REITs)

Investing in income-producing properties such as office buildings, apartments, or retail spaces.

A Real Estate Investment Trust (REIT) is an investment vehicle that allows individuals to invest in a diversified portfolio of income-generating real estate assets. REITs were established in 1960 to give small investors access to real estate investments. They come in three main types: equity REITs, mortgage REITs, and hybrid REITs. Equity REITs generate income from rental properties, while mortgage REITs invest in real estate mortgages and earn revenue from interest payments. Hybrid REITs combine elements of both equity and mortgage REITs.

Investing in REITs offers several benefits. First, it provides diversification as investors can access a range of real estate properties and sectors, reducing risk compared to owning a single property. Additionally, REITs are publicly traded on stock exchanges, providing liquidity and ease of buying and selling. Furthermore, REITs are required to distribute a significant portion of their taxable income as dividends, making them attractive for income-oriented investors. REITs are professionally managed, relieving individual investors from the responsibilities of property management. Lastly, REITs can experience capital appreciation over time, adding potential for growth in addition to dividend income.

Numerous successful REITs have demonstrated consistent returns for investors. For example, Simon Property Group is one of the largest retail REITs, specializing in shopping malls and premium outlets. Prologis, a leading industrial REIT, owns and operates distribution centers and warehouses globally. Equity Residential is a residential REIT that focuses on apartment communities in high-demand markets.

To get involved in REIT investing, there are several options. REITs can be bought and sold through brokerage accounts on stock exchanges. Additionally, investors can gain exposure to a diversified portfolio of REITs through mutual funds or exchange-traded funds (ETFs) that focus on the real estate sector. Private REITs are also available but may have specific requirements, such as minimum investment amounts or accredited investor status. Before investing, thorough research is crucial. Assessing a REIT's performance, track record, investment strategy, and risk profile is essential. Seeking guidance from a financial advisor or investment professional is recommended to align investments with specific financial goals and risk tolerance.

It's important to note that investing in REITs carries risks, including market fluctuations, economic downturns, and changes in real estate values. Investors should carefully consider their investment objectives, conduct due diligence, and be aware of the potential risks before making investment decisions.

Peer-to-Peer Lending

Investing in loans to individuals or businesses through online platforms.

Peer-to-peer lending, also known as P2P lending, has gained significant traction as an alternative form of investing. This innovative financial model enables individuals or businesses to lend and borrow money directly from each other through online platforms, bypassing traditional financial institutions. P2P lending offers an enticing investment opportunity for those seeking higher returns, portfolio diversification, and greater control over their investments.

To grasp the concept of P2P lending, it is essential to understand its mechanics. P2P lending platforms act as intermediaries, connecting lenders and borrowers. Lenders can review borrower profiles and loan requests, assessing factors such as creditworthiness, loan purpose, and interest rates. Once a lending opportunity is identified, lenders can contribute funds to fulfill the loan request. Borrowers, on the other hand, benefit from the ease and accessibility of securing loans through these platforms.

P2P lending encompasses various types of loans. These can range from personal loans for debt consolidation or medical expenses to business loans for expansion or working capital. Each loan request is subject to evaluation, and interest rates are often determined based on the borrower's creditworthiness. This diversity of loan options provides lenders with the opportunity to tailor their investment portfolios according to their risk appetite and investment goals.

In the P2P lending landscape, several key players facilitate the lending process. These include lending platforms, which serve as the virtual marketplace connecting lenders and borrowers. The platforms play a crucial role in vetting borrowers, determining interest rates, and facilitating loan repayment. Additionally, credit bureaus and underwriting algorithms help assess the creditworthiness of borrowers, aiding lenders in making informed investment decisions.

One of the primary advantages of P2P lending is the potential for higher returns compared to traditional investments. With interest rates typically higher than those offered by banks or other investment vehicles, P2P lending presents an opportunity to enhance investment income. Furthermore, P2P lending allows investors to diversify their portfolios beyond traditional asset classes, such as stocks or bonds. This diversification can potentially mitigate risks and enhance overall portfolio performance.

Another benefit of P2P lending is the access to a broader pool of borrowers. Through online platforms, lenders can connect with individuals or businesses seeking funding, even those who may have difficulty obtaining loans through traditional channels. This inclusivity opens up opportunities to support underserved segments of the population and invest in businesses with promising growth prospects.

Transparency and efficiency are key attributes of P2P lending. The online nature of the platforms allows for a transparent process, providing lenders with detailed information about borrowers and their loan requests. Additionally, P2P lending offers a streamlined and efficient experience, eliminating the bureaucratic hurdles often associated with traditional lending institutions.

P2P lending also offers flexibility and control over investments. Lenders have the freedom to choose specific loans they wish to fund, allowing for a personalized investment approach. Moreover, investors can diversify their investment across multiple loans, spreading risk and potentially maximizing returns. The ability to monitor and manage investments in real-time provides a sense of control and involvement that may be lacking in traditional investment avenues.

However, it is crucial to acknowledge the risks and challenges associated with P2P lending. Default risk remains a significant concern, as borrowers may fail to repay their loans, leading to potential financial losses for lenders. Assessing the creditworthiness of borrowers becomes crucial to minimize this risk. Furthermore, the P2P lending industry is still relatively unregulated in many jurisdictions, which raises concerns about investor protection and the lack of standardized practices.

Additionally, P2P lending investments may suffer from illiquidity, as funds are typically tied up for the duration of the loan term. Investors must consider the potential impact of illiquidity on their overall investment strategy and financial needs. Lock-in periods, during which lenders cannot withdraw their funds, further contribute to the illiquid nature of P2P lending investments.

In conclusion, P2P lending presents an exciting avenue for alternative investing, offering attractive returns, diversification opportunities, and greater control over investment portfolios. However, investors must carefully evaluate the risks involved, including default risk, regulatory concerns, and illiquidity. By understanding the mechanics, benefits, and challenges of P2P lending, investors can make informed decisions and potentially capitalize on this evolving form of investment.

Venture Capital:

Investing in early-stage or startup companies with high growth potential.

Venture capital (VC) is a dynamic and exhilarating form of alternative investing that focuses on early-stage or startup companies with significant growth potential. Venture capitalists act as catalysts for these ventures, providing them with capital, expertise, and guidance to nurture them into successful businesses. To fully grasp the world of venture capital, it is crucial to explore its fundamentals, investment strategies, benefits, risks, and key considerations for successful investing.

Venture capital has evolved into a specialized investment approach, targeting companies in their early stages of development. Venture capitalists play a pivotal role in the startup ecosystem, identifying promising ventures, and providing them with the necessary financial resources to grow. This support goes beyond mere funding, as venture capitalists actively engage with the entrepreneurs, offering strategic guidance, mentorship, and access to their extensive networks.

The venture capital investment process involves several stages. Deal sourcing and evaluation form the initial steps, where venture capitalists identify potential investment opportunities through various channels, such as networking events, referrals, or partnerships with incubators and accelerators. Thorough due diligence is then conducted to assess the viability, market potential, and scalability of the startup. Once a favorable investment opportunity is identified, the deal is structured, taking into account factors like valuation, ownership stake, and exit strategies. Post-investment, venture capitalists provide ongoing support to the portfolio companies, leveraging their industry expertise, network, and business acumen to maximize their chances of success.

Venture capital investing offers a range of benefits. One significant advantage is the potential for high growth and capital appreciation. Startups that succeed can experience exponential growth, leading to substantial returns on investment. Additionally, venture capital allows investors to diversify their portfolios and gain exposure to innovative and disruptive technologies, industries, and business models. By investing in startups, venture capitalists contribute to the advancement of cutting-edge ideas and contribute to the evolution of various sectors. Furthermore, venture capitalists have the opportunity to actively participate in the growth and development of portfolio companies, leveraging their expertise and network to add value and influence strategic decisions.

However, venture capital investing is not without risks and challenges. High failure rates among startups are a significant concern, and not all investments will yield positive returns. Illiquidity is another challenge, as venture capital investments often require a long-term commitment, with funds being locked up for several years before potential exits occur. Market volatility and economic conditions can also impact the performance of venture capital investments. Moreover, operational and execution risks within portfolio companies can hinder their growth and ultimately affect investment outcomes.

To navigate the path to successful venture capital investing, several key considerations come into play. Thorough due diligence and market research are essential to evaluate investment opportunities effectively. Constructing a well-diversified portfolio and managing risk through careful selection and allocation of investments is crucial. Building a strong network and establishing relationships with entrepreneurs, fellow investors, and industry experts can provide access to high-quality deals and valuable insights. Patience, a long-term vision, and adaptability are also vital qualities for venture capital investors, as startups require time to mature and pivot based on market dynamics.

Venture capital is not stagnant; it evolves with the ever-changing business landscape. Several trends and innovations shape the industry, including the rise of impact investing, where social and environmental factors are integrated into investment decisions. Emerging technologies and industry focus areas, such as artificial intelligence, blockchain, and biotech, present new investment opportunities. Cross-border investments and global expansion strategies are gaining prominence as startups seek to scale their operations globally. Moreover, the democratization of venture capital through crowdfunding platforms and tokenization is opening up access to a broader range of investors.

In conclusion, venture capital offers a thrilling opportunity for alternative investing, fueling innovation and shaping the entrepreneurial landscape. However, it requires careful analysis, risk management, and active involvement. By understanding the fundamentals of venture capital, investors can navigate the complex ecosystem, seize unique investment opportunities, and contribute to the growth and success of innovative startups.

Private Equity:

Investing in Privately Held Companies

Private equity is a form of alternative investment that involves investing in privately held companies, often with the goal of acquiring a controlling stake. Unlike public equity markets, where shares of publicly traded companies are bought and sold on stock exchanges, private equity investments are made in companies that are not listed on public exchanges. This unique investment approach has gained significant popularity over the years, attracting both institutional investors and high-net-worth individuals seeking diversification and potentially higher returns.

Private equity investments are typically made by private equity firms, also known as financial sponsors. These firms raise capital from institutional investors, such as pension funds, endowments, and insurance companies, as well as from wealthy individuals. The capital raised is then used to invest in privately held companies, with the intention of improving their operations, increasing profitability, and ultimately generating a significant return on investment.

One of the defining characteristics of private equity is the focus on acquiring a controlling stake in the target company. This allows private equity firms to actively influence the strategic direction of the company, often by implementing operational changes, strategic repositioning, or financial restructuring. By taking a hands-on approach, private equity firms aim to unlock the full potential of the invested companies and create value for their investors.

Private equity investments are typically structured as limited partnerships, with the private equity firm acting as the general partner and the institutional investors and high-net-worth individuals as limited partners. The limited partners commit capital to the private equity fund, which is then invested over a specified investment period, typically around five to ten years. During this period, the private equity firm actively manages the portfolio companies and seeks to generate attractive returns.

Private equity investments can take various forms, including leveraged buyouts (LBOs), growth equity investments, and venture capital. Leveraged buyouts involve acquiring a company using a significant amount of debt, with the target company's assets often used as collateral. This strategy allows private equity firms to amplify their returns by using leverage, although it also increases the risk profile of the investment.

Growth equity investments, on the other hand, focus on providing capital to companies that have demonstrated strong growth potential but may need additional resources to fuel their expansion. This type of investment often occurs in more mature companies that are past the early stages of development but still have significant growth opportunities.

Venture capital investments, a subset of private equity, specifically target early-stage companies with high growth potential. These investments are typically made in startups and emerging companies that have innovative business models or technologies. Venture capital firms provide capital, mentorship, and strategic guidance to these companies, with the aim of helping them achieve rapid growth and profitability.

Private equity investments offer several potential benefits for investors. One of the primary attractions is the potential for high returns. By acquiring a controlling stake in a privately held company and actively managing its operations, private equity firms aim to generate substantial value and sell the company at a significantly higher price than the initial investment. This can result in attractive returns, especially if the invested company experiences significant growth or is successfully turned around.

Moreover, private equity investments provide diversification benefits. The returns from private equity are typically uncorrelated with those of public equity markets, meaning they can provide a valuable source of diversification for an investor's overall portfolio. This can help reduce the overall risk of the portfolio and potentially enhance risk-adjusted returns.

Another advantage of private equity is the potential for operational improvements and strategic initiatives. Private equity firms often bring extensive industry expertise and a network of professionals to the table. They work closely with the management teams of the portfolio companies to identify and implement operational efficiencies, strategic partnerships, and other value-enhancing initiatives. This active involvement can contribute to the growth and success of the invested companies.

However, private equity investments also come with certain risks and considerations. One of the primary risks is illiquidity. Unlike publicly traded stocks, private equity investments are not easily bought or sold on a daily basis. Instead, they typically have a long investment horizon, often spanning several years. This illiquidity can restrict investors' ability to access their capital until the private equity fund reaches its predetermined exit strategy, which is often an initial public offering (IPO), sale to another company, or a secondary sale to another private equity firm.

Moreover, private equity investments can be highly complex and require significant due diligence. Evaluating potential investment opportunities, conducting financial analysis, assessing the management team, and negotiating deal terms all require specialized skills and expertise. Investors need to carefully assess the track record and reputation of the private equity firm before committing their capital, as the performance of the fund and the expertise of the team play a crucial role in the success of the investment.

Additionally, private equity investments are subject to market and economic risks. Factors such as changes in interest rates, economic downturns, or industry-specific challenges can impact the performance of portfolio companies and, consequently, the returns generated by the private equity fund. It is essential for investors to understand and evaluate these risks before committing their capital to a private equity investment.

In recent years, private equity has faced increased scrutiny and criticism. Some critics argue that private equity firms prioritize short-term financial gains over the long-term sustainability and well-being of the invested companies. They point to instances of layoffs, cost-cutting measures, and aggressive financial engineering as evidence of this perspective. However, proponents of private equity argue that these measures are necessary to drive operational improvements, enhance efficiency, and position companies for long-term success.

In conclusion, private equity is a form of alternative investment that involves investing in privately held companies with the goal of acquiring a controlling stake. Private equity firms actively manage their portfolio companies, seeking to improve operations, increase profitability, and generate attractive returns for their investors. While private equity investments offer potential benefits such as high returns, diversification, and operational improvements, they also come with risks and considerations, including illiquidity, complexity, and market risks. As with any investment, thorough due diligence and careful evaluation of potential risks and rewards are essential before committing capital to private equity.

Commodities

Investing in Physical Goods

Commodities are an essential component of the global economy, representing tangible physical goods that are widely traded and used in various industries. Investing in commodities provides individuals and institutions with an opportunity to participate in the performance of these essential resources. This form of alternative investing involves buying and selling commodities such as gold, oil, agricultural products, and more. In this article, we will explore the concept of commodity investing, its types, benefits, risks, and the factors that influence commodity prices.

Commodities can be broadly categorized into three main groups: energy, metals, and agriculture. Energy commodities include oil, natural gas, and coal, which are vital for fueling transportation, heating, and electricity generation. Metals such as gold, silver, copper, and platinum are widely used in industries like construction, electronics, and jewelry. Agricultural commodities encompass crops like corn, wheat, soybeans, and livestock products such as cattle, hogs, and poultry.

One of the primary ways to invest in commodities is through the futures market. Futures contracts are standardized agreements to buy or sell a specified quantity of a commodity at a predetermined price and date in the future. Investors can enter into futures contracts to speculate on the price movement of a particular commodity. This approach allows them to gain exposure to commodities without physically owning or storing them.

Investing in commodities through futures contracts offers several advantages. Firstly, futures contracts provide liquidity and ease of trading, as they are actively traded on commodity exchanges worldwide. Investors can enter and exit positions relatively quickly, enabling them to take advantage of price movements. Moreover, futures contracts offer leverage, allowing investors to control a larger quantity of the commodity with a smaller upfront investment. However, leverage can amplify both gains and losses, making futures trading a high-risk strategy.

Apart from futures contracts, investors can also gain exposure to commodities through exchange-traded funds (ETFs) and mutual funds. These investment vehicles pool money from multiple investors to buy a portfolio of commodities or commodity-related securities. Commodities ETFs are designed to track the price performance of specific commodities or commodity indices, allowing investors to participate in the overall commodity market without directly trading futures contracts.

Investing in commodities offers several potential benefits. Firstly, commodities have historically shown low correlation with other asset classes such as stocks and bonds. This low correlation makes commodities an attractive addition to an investment portfolio, as they can provide diversification and potentially reduce overall portfolio risk.

When other investments like stocks or bonds perform poorly, commodities may act as a hedge, helping to offset losses.

Secondly, commodities have the potential to offer inflation protection. In periods of rising inflation, commodity prices tend to increase, as they are influenced by supply and demand dynamics. Investing in commodities can be a way to preserve purchasing power and mitigate the negative effects of inflation on an investment portfolio.

Additionally, commodities are considered a finite resource. As global population and economic growth continue, demand for commodities is expected to rise. This increasing demand, coupled with limited supply, can potentially lead to long-term price appreciation. Investors who believe in the long-term growth prospects of certain commodities may choose to invest in them to capture potential capital appreciation.

However, investing in commodities also carries certain risks and considerations. Firstly, commodity prices can be highly volatile, subject to various factors such as geopolitical events, weather conditions, technological advancements, and changes in global supply and demand. These factors can cause significant price fluctuations, making commodity investing a potentially risky endeavor.

Moreover, commodity investments can be influenced by macroeconomic factors such as currency movements, interest rates, and global economic trends. Changes in these factors can impact commodity prices and investment returns. Investors need to carefully assess and monitor these macroeconomic conditions to make informed investment decisions.

Another risk associated with commodity investing is the storage and transportation costs. Some commodities, like gold or oil, may require storage facilities or transportation infrastructure, which can add additional expenses and logistical challenges. These costs need to be factored into the investment analysis and can affect the overall returns.

Furthermore, investing in commodities requires a good understanding of the specific market dynamics and factors that drive the supply and demand of each commodity. Factors such as weather patterns, government regulations, and technological advancements can significantly impact the performance of individual commodities. Investors need to conduct thorough research and stay informed about these factors to make well-informed investment decisions.

In recent years, the rise of environmental, social, and governance (ESG) considerations has also influenced commodity investing. Investors are increasingly concerned about the sustainability and ethical aspects of investing in certain commodities. For example, concerns about carbon emissions and climate change have led some investors to shy away from investing in fossil fuel commodities like coal or oil. Evaluating the ESG factors and understanding the sustainability implications of commodity investments has become crucial for many investors.

To make informed investment decisions in commodities, investors often rely on various sources of information and analysis. Market reports, industry publications, government data, and expert opinions can provide valuable insights into the supply and demand dynamics, price trends, and other relevant factors affecting commodity markets. Additionally, staying updated on global economic trends, geopolitical events, and policy changes can help investors anticipate potential shifts in commodity prices.

In conclusion, commodities offer investors an opportunity to participate in the performance of essential physical goods. Investing in commodities can provide diversification, inflation protection, and the potential for long-term capital appreciation. However, commodity investing comes with risks such as price volatility, macroeconomic factors, storage costs, and the need for specialized market knowledge. Investors should carefully evaluate these risks and consider their investment goals, risk tolerance, and time horizon before venturing into commodity investments. Additionally, staying informed and conducting thorough research are essential to navigate the complex and ever-changing world of commodity investing.

Cryptocurrencies:

Investing in Digital Currencies

Cryptocurrencies have revolutionized the world of finance and investment by introducing digital currencies that operate on decentralized networks using cryptographic technology. Investing in cryptocurrencies involves buying and holding digital assets like Bitcoin, Ethereum, or Litecoin, with the hope of generating a return on investment. This form of alternative investing has gained significant attention and popularity in recent years, attracting individuals, institutions, and even governments. In this article, we will explore the concept of cryptocurrency investing, its types, benefits, risks, and the factors that influence cryptocurrency prices.

Cryptocurrencies are digital or virtual currencies that utilize cryptography for secure transactions and to control the creation of new units. Unlike traditional fiat currencies issued by central banks, cryptocurrencies operate on decentralized networks called blockchains. Blockchains are distributed ledgers that record and verify transactions across multiple computers or nodes, ensuring transparency, security, and immutability.

Bitcoin, introduced in 2009, was the first cryptocurrency and remains the most well-known and widely used. It paved the way for the development of thousands of other cryptocurrencies, often referred to as altcoins. Ethereum, Litecoin, Ripple, and Bitcoin Cash are among the most prominent altcoins, each with its own unique features and use cases.

Investing in cryptocurrencies can be done in various ways. The most straightforward method is to buy cryptocurrencies on cryptocurrency exchanges. These platforms facilitate the buying and selling of cryptocurrencies in exchange for traditional fiat currencies or other cryptocurrencies. Investors can create accounts, deposit funds, and purchase cryptocurrencies at prevailing market prices. The acquired cryptocurrencies can then be stored in digital wallets, which are software applications that securely store private keys required to access and transfer the digital assets.

Cryptocurrency investments can also be made through initial coin offerings (ICOs) or token sales. ICOs are crowdfunding events in which projects or companies issue their own tokens or coins to raise capital. Investors can participate in ICOs by purchasing these tokens, often at discounted prices compared to future market prices. However, ICOs carry higher risks, as they are often associated with early-stage projects and regulatory uncertainties.

Furthermore, cryptocurrency investments can be made through mining. Mining involves validating and recording transactions on a blockchain network by solving complex mathematical problems. Miners are rewarded with newly created cryptocurrency units as an incentive for their computational efforts. However, mining has become increasingly resource-intensive and specialized, often requiring significant investments in hardware and electricity.

Investing in cryptocurrencies offers several potential benefits. Firstly, cryptocurrencies have shown the potential for substantial returns. Historically, cryptocurrencies like Bitcoin have experienced significant price appreciation, creating opportunities for investors to generate substantial profits. However, it's important to note that the cryptocurrency market is highly volatile, and prices can fluctuate dramatically in short periods.

Secondly, cryptocurrencies provide diversification for investment portfolios. Due to their low correlation with traditional asset classes like stocks and bonds, cryptocurrencies can help reduce portfolio risk. Adding cryptocurrencies to a diversified investment portfolio may enhance overall returns and provide a hedge against market downturns.

Additionally, cryptocurrencies offer accessibility and inclusivity. Traditional financial systems often have barriers to entry, such as minimum investment requirements, geographical limitations, or complex regulatory processes. Cryptocurrencies, on the other hand, are accessible to anyone with an internet connection, allowing individuals worldwide to participate in the global financial system.

Moreover, cryptocurrencies enable faster and cheaper cross-border transactions. Traditional remittance services can be slow, expensive, and subject to intermediaries. Cryptocurrencies provide an alternative, allowing for near-instantaneous peer-to-peer transactions with reduced fees.

However, investing in cryptocurrencies also carries certain risks and considerations. The cryptocurrency market is known for its high volatility, with prices capable of experiencing significant fluctuations in short periods. This volatility can lead to substantial gains but can also result in substantial losses. Investors should carefully assess their risk tolerance and be prepared for the inherent price volatility when investing in cryptocurrencies.

Furthermore, the cryptocurrency market is relatively young and less regulated compared to traditional financial markets. This lack of regulation can expose investors to scams, frauds, and market manipulation. It is crucial for investors to conduct thorough due diligence and exercise caution when selecting cryptocurrency exchanges, wallets, and investment opportunities.

Additionally, cybersecurity risks are prevalent in the cryptocurrency space. Hacks, thefts, and fraudulent activities targeting cryptocurrency exchanges and wallets have occurred in the past, resulting in the loss of significant amounts of digital assets. Investors must prioritize security by utilizing reputable exchanges, implementing strong passwords, enabling two-factor authentication, and storing cryptocurrencies in secure wallets.

Moreover, the regulatory landscape surrounding cryptocurrencies is evolving. Different countries have adopted varying approaches to regulate cryptocurrencies, ranging from supportive and progressive to restrictive or even outright bans. Regulatory changes can impact the cryptocurrency market and investor sentiment, making it essential for investors to stay informed about regulatory developments.

Furthermore, the technological risks associated with cryptocurrencies should be considered. While blockchain technology has proven to be robust, there are risks related to software bugs, protocol vulnerabilities, and scalability limitations. Investors should evaluate the underlying technology and assess the long-term viability and potential risks associated with the cryptocurrencies they invest in.

In conclusion, investing in cryptocurrencies offers individuals and institutions the opportunity to participate in the evolving digital financial ecosystem. Cryptocurrencies provide potential for significant returns, diversification benefits, accessibility, and faster cross-border transactions. However, cryptocurrency investments come with risks such as high volatility, regulatory uncertainties, cybersecurity threats, and technological risks. Investors should carefully evaluate these risks, conduct thorough research, and seek professional advice before venturing into cryptocurrency investments. Additionally, staying informed about market developments, technological advancements, and regulatory changes is crucial for successful cryptocurrency investing.

Art and Collectibles

Investing in Valuable Assets

Art and collectibles are tangible assets that have a unique appeal to investors. Investing in valuable artwork, antiques, rare stamps, or coins is a form of alternative investing that combines passion for aesthetics and cultural value with the potential for financial returns. This article will explore the concept of art and collectible investing, its types, benefits, risks, and factors that influence the value of these assets.

Art and collectibles encompass a wide range of objects that possess aesthetic, historical, or cultural significance. Artworks can include paintings, sculptures, photographs, and installations created by renowned artists. Collectibles can include a diverse array of items such as antiques, rare stamps, coins, vintage cars, jewelry, sports memorabilia, and more. The value of these assets often goes beyond their material worth, as they are coveted for their historical context, rarity, craftsmanship, and cultural significance.

Investing in art and collectibles can be done through various methods. One approach is direct ownership, where investors purchase artworks or collectibles outright. They can acquire these assets through galleries, auction houses, dealers, or private transactions. The acquired pieces can be displayed, stored, or loaned to museums for exhibitions, offering personal enjoyment and potential appreciation in value over time.

Another method of investing in art and collectibles is through investment funds or partnerships. These pooled investment vehicles allow investors to collectively own a portfolio of artworks or collectibles. Investment funds often employ experts in the field who curate and manage the portfolio, making investment decisions on behalf of the investors. This approach provides investors with diversified exposure to a range of assets, mitigating the risks associated with owning individual pieces.

One of the key attractions of art and collectible investing is the potential for significant returns. Over time, certain artworks and collectibles have shown the ability to appreciate in value, sometimes substantially. The scarcity and uniqueness of these assets, coupled with increasing demand from collectors and institutions, can drive their prices upward. Investing in highly sought-after pieces or collectibles with a strong historical or cultural significance can potentially yield substantial financial gains.

Moreover, art and collectible investments offer diversification benefits. These assets often have a low correlation with traditional financial markets, such as stocks and bonds. The value of artworks and collectibles can be influenced by factors independent of broader economic conditions. Therefore, including art and collectibles in an investment portfolio can help reduce overall portfolio risk and enhance risk-adjusted returns.

Furthermore, investing in art and collectibles can provide personal enjoyment and fulfillment. Unlike many other investment assets, artworks and collectibles offer aesthetic pleasure and cultural value. Collectors often develop a deep appreciation for the beauty, historical context, and craftsmanship of the objects they acquire. This emotional connection and the ability to engage with the collection can make the investment experience more fulfilling.

However, investing in art and collectibles also comes with risks and considerations. One of the primary risks is the subjective nature of valuing these assets. The value of artworks and collectibles is highly dependent on factors such as artist reputation, condition, rarity, provenance, and market demand. Valuation can be challenging and subjective, and it requires expertise and experience to accurately assess the worth of an artwork or collectible. Market trends and shifts in tastes can significantly impact the value of these assets, making them susceptible to volatility.

Additionally, art and collectibles face risks related to authenticity and provenance. Due to their unique nature, these assets can be vulnerable to fraud or forgery. Thorough due diligence is necessary to ensure the authenticity and legitimacy of the artworks or collectibles being acquired. Verifying provenance, consulting experts, and conducting comprehensive research are essential steps in mitigating these risks.

Furthermore, art and collectible investments can be illiquid. Unlike stocks or bonds, which can be readily bought or sold on exchanges, selling an artwork or collectible often requires finding a suitable buyer through private sales, auctions, or specialized dealers. The process of finding a buyer and completing a transaction can take time and may not guarantee immediate liquidity. Investors need to consider their liquidity needs and have a long-term investment horizon when investing in art and collectibles.

Another risk associated with art and collectible investments is the potential for damage, loss, or theft. These assets are fragile and require proper storage, handling, and insurance. Adequate security measures should be in place to protect the collection from physical damage or theft. Additionally, preserving the condition of artworks and collectibles is crucial to maintaining their value over time.

In recent years, the emergence of online platforms and blockchain technology has aimed to address some of the challenges in the art and collectible market. Online marketplaces and platforms have increased accessibility, transparency, and liquidity for buyers and sellers. Blockchain technology offers the potential for enhanced provenance verification and authenticity assurance, reducing the risks associated with forgeries and frauds.

In conclusion, investing in art and collectibles provides an opportunity to combine aesthetic appreciation with the potential for financial returns. These tangible assets offer potential appreciation in value, diversification benefits, personal enjoyment, and cultural value. However, investing in art and collectibles requires expertise, thorough research, and careful consideration of risks such as valuation challenges, authenticity concerns, illiquidity, and security. Investors should approach this form of alternative investment with a long-term perspective, an understanding of the market dynamics, and a willingness to engage in the cultural and historical context of the assets they acquire.

Angel Investing:

Fueling Early-Stage Ventures

Angel investing is a form of alternative investing that involves providing capital to early-stage companies in exchange for equity. Angel investors, also known as private investors or seed investors, play a vital role in supporting the growth and development of innovative startups. This article will explore the concept of angel investing, its benefits, risks, strategies, and the evolving landscape of this dynamic investment approach.

Angel investing refers to the practice of investing personal funds or pooled capital into promising early-stage companies. These companies are typically in their initial stages of development and may lack sufficient access to traditional forms of funding, such as bank loans or venture capital. Angel investors bridge this funding gap by providing financial support and strategic guidance to help these startups succeed.

Angel investments are made in a wide range of industries, including technology, healthcare, consumer goods, clean energy, and more. The companies seeking angel investment often have a high growth potential, innovative business models, or disruptive technologies. By investing in these early-stage ventures, angel investors aim to generate a significant return on investment in the long run.

One of the primary motivations for angel investing is the potential for substantial financial returns. Early-stage investments carry higher risks compared to more established companies but also offer the possibility of significant rewards. Angel investors typically aim to identify companies with the potential to achieve rapid growth and increase in valuation. If the invested company successfully scales its operations and eventually exits through an acquisition or an initial public offering (IPO), angel investors can realize substantial capital gains.

Furthermore, angel investing provides angel investors with the opportunity to support entrepreneurs and contribute to the development of innovative ideas. Many angel investors are experienced entrepreneurs or industry professionals who bring not only capital but also valuable knowledge, expertise, and networks to the table. They act as mentors, advisors, and connectors, assisting startups in navigating challenges, refining their business strategies, and accessing additional resources.

Angel investing also offers the potential for diversification in an investment portfolio. By allocating a portion of their capital to early-stage ventures, angel investors can diversify their overall investment risk. The returns from angel investments are typically uncorrelated with traditional asset classes such as stocks or bonds, providing a potential source of diversification and potentially enhancing risk-adjusted returns.

Angel investments can be structured in various ways. The most common form is equity financing, where angel investors provide capital to the startup in exchange for a percentage of ownership or equity stake. Angel investors and entrepreneurs negotiate the terms of the investment, including the valuation of the company, the amount of equity to be issued, and any additional rights or preferences attached to the shares.

Another investment approach used by angel investors is convertible debt or convertible notes. Convertible debt is a form of short-term loan that can be converted into equity at a later stage, usually when the company raises a subsequent round of financing. This structure provides flexibility to the investor, allowing them to convert their debt into equity at a predetermined valuation or receive repayment of the loan with interest.

Angel investing is not without risks. Early-stage investments carry a high degree of uncertainty and a higher likelihood of failure compared to more mature companies. Many startups fail to achieve profitability or secure subsequent funding rounds, resulting in a total loss of the angel investment. Angel investors must carefully assess the investment opportunities, conduct thorough due diligence, and evaluate the startup's business model, market potential, team, and competitive landscape.

Additionally, angel investors face liquidity challenges. Unlike publicly traded stocks, angel investments are illiquid and may require a long holding period. Startups typically take several years to develop and grow, and exits through acquisitions or IPOs are relatively rare. Angel investors should be prepared for a more extended investment horizon and consider the illiquid nature of their investments when managing their overall investment portfolio.

To mitigate the risks and increase the chances of success, angel investors often employ specific strategies. They focus on building diversified portfolios by investing in multiple startups across different industries and stages of development. This diversification spreads the risk and increases the likelihood of having successful investments that outweigh the potential losses.

Moreover, angel investors leverage their networks and industry expertise to identify investment opportunities, conduct due diligence, and support the growth of the invested companies. They often join angel networks or syndicates, which allow them to pool their capital, share insights, and collaborate on investment decisions. These networks provide access to a broader range of investment opportunities and increase the chances of successful investments through collective knowledge and resources.

The landscape of angel investing has evolved significantly in recent years. With advancements in technology and communication, angel investors now have access to a broader pool of investment opportunities beyond their local geographic regions. Online platforms and crowdfunding have facilitated the democratization of angel investing, allowing individuals to invest smaller amounts in startups and participate in the early-stage investment ecosystem.

Additionally, the emergence of angel investor groups, accelerators, and incubators has provided startups with additional support and resources.

These organizations help identify and nurture promising startups, providing access to mentorship, education, funding, and networking opportunities. They play a crucial role in bridging the gap between angel investors and entrepreneurs, facilitating the flow of capital and knowledge.

In recent years, angel investing has also become an area of interest for institutional investors, such as venture capital firms, family offices, and corporate venture arms. These entities recognize the potential of early-stage investments and allocate dedicated funds or resources to participate in angel investing. This trend has increased the competition for investment opportunities and influenced the dynamics of angel investing.

In conclusion, angel investing offers a unique opportunity for investors to support early-stage companies and potentially generate significant financial returns. Angel investors provide capital, expertise, and mentorship to startups, helping them navigate the challenges of scaling their businesses. While angel investing carries risks, including high failure rates and illiquidity, proper due diligence, diversification, and leveraging networks can enhance the chances of success. With the evolving landscape and increasing accessibility of angel investing, more individuals and institutions are participating in this dynamic form of alternative investing.

Film Financing:

Investing in the Production of Films and Television Shows

Film financing is a unique form of alternative investing that involves providing capital for the production of films, documentaries, or television shows. Investors in the film industry contribute financial resources to support the creation, marketing, and distribution of visual content. This article will explore the concept of film financing, its types, benefits, risks, and the factors that influence the success of film investments.

Film financing encompasses a range of investment opportunities within the entertainment industry. It can involve financing independent films, co-producing television shows, funding documentaries, or supporting the production of big-budget Hollywood movies. Investors in the film industry play a crucial role in bringing creative visions to life and capitalizing on the commercial success of visual content.

One of the primary methods of film financing is equity investment. Equity investors provide capital in exchange for ownership or equity stakes in the film or production company. These investors participate in the financial success of the project through profit sharing or potential capital appreciation. Equity investors typically contribute a significant portion of the project's budget and may have a say in creative decisions or business strategies.

Another common method of film financing is debt financing. Debt investors provide loans to the production company or filmmakers, which are repaid with interest over a specified period. These loans may be secured against the film's future revenue or collateralized by other assets. Debt financing allows filmmakers to access capital without diluting ownership or control but requires repayment regardless of the project's commercial success.

Additionally, film financing can involve the sale of distribution rights or pre-sales agreements. Distribution companies or international distributors may acquire the rights to distribute the film in specific regions or territories. Pre-sales agreements involve selling the film's rights to distributors or broadcasters before the production is completed, providing upfront financing to cover production costs. These agreements can help reduce the financial risks associated with film production by securing guaranteed revenue streams.

Film financing offers several potential benefits for investors. Firstly, the film industry has the potential for significant financial returns. Successful films can generate substantial profits through box office revenues, international sales, licensing deals, merchandising, and digital distribution platforms. Investors who back commercially successful films can realize substantial returns on their investments.

Moreover, film investments offer diversification benefits. The film industry operates independently of traditional financial markets and can provide a valuable source of diversification for investment portfolios. The performance of films and the success of the film industry are influenced by different factors than those affecting stocks or bonds. Including film investments can potentially enhance risk-adjusted returns and reduce overall portfolio risk.

Furthermore, film financing allows investors to support creative endeavors and contribute to the cultural landscape. Filmmakers often use storytelling as a means of exploring important social issues, sharing diverse perspectives, and creating memorable experiences for audiences. Film investors can play a role in promoting artistic expression and supporting emerging talents.

However, film financing also comes with risks and considerations. Investing in the film industry carries a high degree of uncertainty and can be challenging to predict commercial success. The financial performance of films can be influenced by various factors, including competition, changing consumer preferences, marketing strategies, critical reception, and economic conditions. Investors must conduct thorough due diligence, evaluate the track record and experience of the filmmakers, and assess the potential market demand for the project.

Furthermore, the film industry is characterized by a "hit-driven" model, where a small number of successful films generate a significant portion of the industry's profits. The majority of films may not achieve commercial success, resulting in financial losses for investors. Investors need to carefully manage their risk exposure and diversify their film investments to mitigate the impact of potential failures.

Additionally, film investments are illiquid and can have long investment horizons. The production, marketing, and distribution of films often span several years, and returns on investment may not materialize until after the film's release and subsequent revenue generation. Investors must consider their liquidity needs and have a long-term investment outlook when investing in the film industry.

To mitigate risks and increase the chances of success, film investors often employ strategies such as investing in a portfolio of films, diversifying across genres or production budgets, and partnering with experienced production companies or filmmakers. Partnering with reputable production companies can provide access to high-quality projects, experienced teams, and established distribution networks, increasing the chances of commercial success.

Furthermore, the growth of digital distribution platforms and streaming services has transformed the film industry's landscape. These platforms have created new opportunities for independent filmmakers, allowing films to reach global audiences without traditional distribution channels. Investors should consider the evolving distribution landscape and assess the potential impact of digital platforms on revenue streams and financial returns.

In conclusion, film financing offers investors a unique opportunity to support the production of films, documentaries, or television shows while potentially generating financial returns. Film investments can provide significant profits, diversification benefits, and the satisfaction of contributing to the cultural landscape. However, investing in the film industry carries risks related to commercial success, changing market dynamics, and long investment horizons. Thorough due diligence, diversification, and partnering with experienced teams are crucial for managing these risks. By carefully assessing investment opportunities, understanding the film industry's dynamics, and staying informed about market trends, film investors can position themselves for potential success in this dynamic and creative sector.

Structured Settlement Investments:

Investing in Future Payments from Lawsuits and Insurance Settlements

Structured settlement investments are a unique form of alternative investing that involves purchasing the rights to future payments from personal injury lawsuits or insurance settlements. Structured settlements provide a way for individuals to receive periodic payments over time rather than a lump sum. However, some recipients may prefer to access their funds immediately. Investors can step in by purchasing the structured settlement payment rights at a discounted rate, providing immediate liquidity to the recipient. This article will explore the concept of structured settlement investments, their benefits, risks, regulatory considerations, and factors that influence investment decisions.

Structured settlements are financial arrangements typically used to settle personal injury lawsuits, medical malpractice claims, or insurance disputes. Instead of receiving a one-time lump sum payment, the recipient agrees to periodic payments over a specified period. These payments are designed to cover medical expenses, ongoing care, lost wages, or other financial needs resulting from the settlement.

Structured settlement investments involve purchasing some or all of the future payment rights from the recipient of the structured settlement. Investors, often referred to as factoring companies or structured settlement purchasers, offer a discounted lump sum payment to the recipient in exchange for the right to receive the future payments. The discount is based on several factors, including the amount and timing of the payments, prevailing interest rates, and the investor's assessment of the investment's risk and return.

One of the primary motivations for structured settlement investments is the potential for financial gain. Investors in structured settlements seek to profit by purchasing the future payment rights at a discounted rate and receiving the periodic payments over time. This discounted rate allows investors to benefit from the time value of money, as they receive a larger amount than the initial investment when considering the present value of the future payments.

Structured settlement investments also provide liquidity to individuals who may need immediate access to their funds. Personal circumstances or financial needs may arise that make receiving a lump sum payment more desirable than waiting for periodic payments. Selling a portion or all of the structured settlement payments allows recipients to access a significant amount of cash upfront, which can be used to pay off debts, invest in other ventures, or address immediate financial needs.

Furthermore, structured settlement investments offer diversification benefits for investors. Structured settlements have a low correlation with traditional financial assets such as stocks or bonds. Investing in structured settlements can help investors diversify their portfolios and potentially reduce overall investment risk. The performance of structured settlement investments is influenced by factors different from those affecting traditional investments, providing an alternative source of returns.

However, structured settlement investments also carry risks and considerations. The primary risk for investors is the potential for default or non-payment of the structured settlement payments. If the individual responsible for making the payments, such as an insurance company, becomes insolvent or fails to fulfill its obligations, investors may not receive the expected future payments. Proper due diligence, including assessing the creditworthiness and financial stability of the payer, is crucial to mitigating this risk.

Additionally, structured settlement investments may involve legal and regulatory complexities. In some jurisdictions, the sale of structured settlement payment rights is subject to specific laws and regulations designed to protect the recipient's interests. Investors must comply with applicable laws, including obtaining court approval for the transaction in some cases. Legal counsel or professional advice is often sought to ensure compliance with the relevant regulations.

Furthermore, the discount rate applied to structured settlement investments is an important consideration. The discount rate represents the investor's expected rate of return and accounts for the time value of money, risk factors, and liquidity considerations. Determining an appropriate discount rate requires careful analysis of the specific structured settlement, prevailing interest rates, and the investor's risk appetite.

It is essential to note that investing in structured settlements may not be suitable for all investors. Structured settlement investments typically involve long-term commitments, as the periodic payments extend over an extended period. Investors should carefully consider their investment horizon, liquidity needs, and financial goals before entering into structured settlement investment transactions.

The structured settlement investment industry has evolved over time, driven by changes in regulations, investor demand, and market dynamics. Various industry associations and professional organizations have emerged to establish best practices and promote ethical conduct within the structured settlement industry. These organizations provide resources, guidelines, and educational materials to help investors navigate the complexities of structured settlement investments.

Additionally, the rise of secondary markets and online platforms has increased the accessibility of structured settlement investments. These platforms connect investors with structured settlement sellers, streamlining the transaction process and providing a marketplace for buyers and sellers to engage in structured settlement investment transactions. Online platforms often offer tools and resources to assist investors in evaluating investment opportunities and assessing the risks and benefits associated with structured settlement investments.

In conclusion, structured settlement investments offer a unique alternative investment opportunity that involves purchasing future payment rights from personal injury lawsuits or insurance settlements. These investments provide potential financial gain for investors while offering liquidity to recipients who prefer immediate access to their funds. Structured settlement investments provide diversification benefits and an alternative source of returns. However, investors must carefully assess the risks, regulatory considerations, and financial implications associated with structured settlement investments. Seeking professional advice and conducting thorough due diligence are crucial steps in navigating the structured settlement investment landscape and making informed investment decisions.

Renewable Energy:

Investing in Clean Energy Projects

Renewable energy investment is a rapidly growing form of alternative investing that focuses on financing clean energy projects such as solar farms, wind farms, hydropower plants, and geothermal installations. These investments support the transition from fossil fuel-based energy sources to sustainable and environmentally friendly alternatives. This article will explore the concept of renewable energy investing, its types, benefits, risks, regulatory considerations, and the factors that influence investment decisions.

Renewable energy investments involve allocating capital to projects that generate energy from renewable sources. The global shift towards clean energy has gained momentum due to concerns about climate change, the depletion of fossil fuel reserves, and the increasing demand for sustainable energy solutions. Investing in renewable energy allows individuals, institutions, and governments to contribute to a cleaner and more sustainable future while potentially generating attractive financial returns.

One of the primary methods of renewable energy investing is project financing. Investors provide capital to fund the development, construction, and operation of renewable energy projects. These projects can include solar farms, where sunlight is converted into electricity using photovoltaic panels, or wind farms that harness the power of wind to generate electricity through wind turbines. Other forms of renewable energy projects include hydropower plants that utilize flowing water, geothermal installations that tap into the Earth's heat, and biomass facilities that convert organic materials into energy.

Renewable energy project financing typically involves a combination of debt and equity investments. Debt investors, such as banks or specialized renewable energy lenders, provide loans to fund a portion of the project costs. These loans are secured by the project's assets and cash flows. Equity investors, on the other hand, contribute capital in exchange for an ownership stake in the project. They participate in the project's financial returns and can influence strategic decisions.

Renewable energy investments offer several benefits to investors. Firstly, they provide the opportunity to generate stable and attractive financial returns. Renewable energy projects often have long-term power purchase agreements (PPAs) in place, ensuring a predictable revenue stream over an extended period. These PPAs guarantee that the project's generated electricity is sold at a fixed price to utility companies or other off-takers. Investors can benefit from the stable cash flows and potential capital appreciation associated with renewable energy projects.

Moreover, investing in renewable energy contributes to the mitigation of climate change and the reduction of greenhouse gas emissions. Renewable energy sources produce electricity without the harmful environmental impact associated with fossil fuels. By investing in clean energy projects, investors support the global effort to transition to a low-carbon economy and mitigate the negative effects of climate change.

Additionally, renewable energy investments offer diversification benefits. The performance of renewable energy projects is often uncorrelated with traditional financial markets, such as stocks or bonds. Investing in renewable energy can help diversify an investment portfolio and reduce exposure to risks associated with fossil fuel-dependent industries. The global demand for clean energy continues to grow, creating opportunities for investors to benefit from the long-term trends in the renewable energy sector.

Furthermore, renewable energy investments provide job creation and local economic development. The development and construction of renewable energy projects require skilled labor, creating employment opportunities in local communities. These projects also generate tax revenues and contribute to the local economy through the purchase of goods and services. Investing in renewable energy can have a positive social impact by supporting sustainable economic growth and community development.

However, renewable energy investments also carry risks and considerations. One of the primary risks is the variability of renewable energy resource availability. Solar and wind energy generation, for example, are dependent on weather conditions and can be intermittent. While technological advancements and forecasting techniques have improved the predictability of renewable energy production, fluctuations in energy generation can impact the financial performance of projects. Investors must assess the resource potential and the associated risks of specific renewable energy projects.

Moreover, regulatory and policy changes can significantly influence the renewable energy sector. Government incentives, subsidies, feed-in tariffs, and renewable portfolio standards can impact the financial viability of renewable energy projects. Changes in regulatory frameworks or political support for clean energy can create uncertainties and affect project revenues. Investors need to stay informed about relevant policies and regulations and assess the potential impact on their renewable energy investments.

Additionally, financing renewable energy projects requires specialized knowledge and expertise. Investors need to understand the technical aspects of renewable energy technologies, project development processes, and financial modeling specific to the sector. Conducting thorough due diligence, assessing project feasibility, and working with experienced partners are crucial steps in managing the risks associated with renewable energy investments.

Furthermore, the scalability and cost competitiveness of renewable energy technologies are essential factors to consider. The cost of renewable energy technologies, such as solar panels and wind turbines, has significantly decreased in recent years, making them more economically viable. Investors should assess the potential for cost reductions, technological advancements, and economies of scale in the renewable energy sector.

The renewable energy investment landscape has evolved significantly in recent years. The growth of specialized renewable energy funds, project developers, and investment platforms has increased the accessibility of renewable energy investments. Institutional investors, such as pension funds and sovereign wealth funds, have also become prominent players in the renewable energy space, allocating significant

Farmland Investing:

Acquiring Agricultural Land for Farming or Leasing Purposes

Farmland investing is a form of alternative investing that involves acquiring agricultural land for farming or leasing purposes. Investing in farmland provides individuals, institutions, and even governments with an opportunity to participate in the agricultural sector and potentially generate financial returns. This article will explore the concept of farmland investing, its types, benefits, risks, sustainability considerations, and factors that influence investment decisions.

Farmland investing involves the acquisition of agricultural land for various purposes, including farming operations, leasing to farmers, or holding for potential future development. Agricultural land is an essential asset in the global food production system, supporting the cultivation of crops, livestock grazing, and other agricultural activities. Investing in farmland allows investors to participate in the agricultural sector, which is vital for food security, economic development, and environmental sustainability.

There are different methods of farmland investing, each with its own considerations. One approach is direct ownership, where investors purchase and manage farmland themselves. This involves acquiring land, selecting suitable crops or livestock, managing agricultural operations, and potentially selling agricultural products directly. Direct ownership provides investors with direct control over the land and farming activities, allowing them to capture the full value generated from agricultural operations.

Another method of farmland investing is through farmland investment funds or partnerships. These investment vehicles pool capital from multiple investors and use it to acquire and manage farmland portfolios. Farmland investment funds are typically managed by experienced professionals who oversee land selection, agricultural operations, and overall investment strategies. Investing through funds allows investors to access diversified farmland portfolios and benefit from professional expertise and economies of scale.

Farmland can also be leased to farmers, providing an income stream for investors without the need for direct involvement in farming operations. Lease arrangements can take various forms, such as cash rent leases, crop share leases, or custom farming agreements. In cash rent leases, the farmer pays a fixed rental amount for the use of the land. In crop share leases, the farmer shares a portion of the crop yield with the landowner. Custom farming agreements involve the landowner contracting with a farmer to perform specific farming operations in exchange for a fee. Leasing farmland can provide steady income and potentially diversify investment returns.

Farmland investments offer several benefits to investors. Firstly, farmland has the potential for capital appreciation. Over the long term, well-managed farmland can increase in value due to factors such as population growth, increased food demand, urbanization, and limited supply of agricultural land. Farmland investments can provide a hedge against inflation and potentially generate attractive returns.

Moreover, farmland investments offer income generation through agricultural operations or leasing arrangements. Agricultural land can produce various crops, livestock, or other agricultural products, generating regular income for investors. Leasing farmland to farmers provides a passive income stream without the need for direct involvement in agricultural operations.

Additionally, investing in farmland can offer diversification benefits. Farmland investments have a low correlation with traditional financial assets, such as stocks or bonds. The performance of farmland is influenced by factors unique to the agricultural sector, including weather conditions, commodity prices, global trade dynamics, and policy changes. Including farmland investments in an investment portfolio can help reduce overall portfolio risk and enhance risk-adjusted returns.

Furthermore, farmland investments support sustainable agriculture and environmental stewardship. Sustainable farming practices, such as organic farming, regenerative agriculture, and precision agriculture, aim to minimize environmental impact, conserve natural resources, and promote soil health. Investing in farmland provides capital to support these practices, contributing to sustainable food production and land conservation efforts.

However, farmland investments also carry risks and considerations. The agricultural sector is exposed to various risks, including weather events, pests and diseases, commodity price volatility, and policy changes. Investors must assess these risks and factor them into their investment decisions. Diversification across different regions, crop types, and farming systems can help mitigate risks associated with specific factors.

Moreover, farmland investments require specialized knowledge and expertise. Understanding agricultural markets, crop selection, farming practices, soil management, water availability, and regulatory frameworks is crucial for successful farmland investing. Investors often partner with agricultural experts, farm management companies, or agricultural consultants to navigate these complexities and optimize their investments.

Additionally, farmland investments may face challenges related to liquidity. Agricultural land is considered a relatively illiquid asset, meaning it may take time to find suitable buyers or tenants if the investor decides to sell or lease the land. Investors should consider their liquidity needs and have a long-term investment horizon when investing in farmland.

Sustainability considerations are increasingly important in farmland investing. Investors are recognizing the need to support sustainable agriculture practices that promote environmental stewardship, soil conservation, water management, and biodiversity preservation. Integrating environmental, social, and governance (ESG) factors into farmland investment decisions can help identify opportunities that align with sustainability goals and mitigate potential risks.

Farmland investments can also have a social impact by supporting local economies and rural communities. Agriculture is a vital economic sector in many regions, providing employment opportunities and contributing to local economic development. Investing in farmland can help sustain agricultural livelihoods and support rural communities.

In conclusion, farmland investing provides an opportunity to participate in the agricultural sector and potentially generate financial returns. Farmland investments offer benefits such as capital appreciation, income generation, diversification, and alignment with sustainability goals. However, investing in farmland requires specialized knowledge, careful risk assessment

Wine and Fine Spirits:

Investing in Rare and Collectible Assets

Investing in rare and collectible wines or spirits is a fascinating form of alternative investing that combines the pleasure of connoisseurship with the potential for financial returns. Wine and fine spirits have a unique allure and cultural significance, making them desirable assets for collectors and investors alike. This article will explore the concept of wine and fine spirits investing, its types, benefits, risks, factors influencing value, and strategies for successful investment.

Wine and fine spirits investing involves acquiring and holding rare and collectible bottles for potential appreciation in value over time. These investments go beyond the enjoyment of drinking the beverage, as they focus on the inherent value, historical significance, and scarcity of the bottles themselves. Collectors and investors in this space are passionate about the craftsmanship, provenance, and unique qualities that make certain wines and spirits highly sought after.

One of the key attractions of wine and fine spirits investing is the potential for significant returns. Over time, certain rare and collectible bottles have shown the ability to appreciate in value, sometimes substantially. The scarcity, age, quality, and provenance of these assets, coupled with increasing demand from collectors, connoisseurs, and enthusiasts, can drive their prices upward. Investing in highly sought-after wines or spirits with a strong track record of value appreciation can potentially yield substantial financial gains.

Moreover, wine and fine spirits investments offer diversification benefits. These assets have a low correlation with traditional financial markets, such as stocks and bonds. The value of wines and spirits can be influenced by factors independent of broader economic conditions. Including wine and fine spirits investments in an investment portfolio can help reduce overall portfolio risk and enhance risk-adjusted returns.

Additionally, investing in wine and fine spirits can provide personal enjoyment and fulfillment. Unlike many other investment assets, rare and collectible bottles offer aesthetic pleasure, cultural value, and the opportunity to appreciate the craftsmanship and history of the beverage. Collectors often develop a deep appreciation for the taste profiles, regions, vintages, and aging potential of the wines or spirits they acquire. This emotional connection and the ability to savor and share the collection can make the investment experience more enriching.

However, wine and fine spirits investing also come with risks and considerations. One of the primary risks is the subjective nature of valuing these assets. The value of rare and collectible wines and spirits is highly dependent on factors such as brand reputation, vintage, condition, rarity, provenance, and market demand. Valuation can be challenging and subjective, requiring expertise and experience to accurately assess the worth of a particular bottle or collection. Market trends and shifts in tastes can significantly impact the value of these assets, making them susceptible to volatility.

Additionally, wine and fine spirits face risks related to authenticity and provenance. Due to their desirability, these assets can be vulnerable to fraud or counterfeiting. Thorough due diligence is necessary to ensure the authenticity and legitimacy of the bottles being acquired. Verifying provenance, consulting experts, and conducting comprehensive research are essential steps in mitigating these risks.

Furthermore, wine and fine spirits investments require proper storage and handling to maintain their quality and value. These assets are sensitive to temperature, humidity, light exposure, and vibration. Investing in suitable storage facilities or working with professional storage services is crucial to preserve the condition and value of the collection over time.

Market knowledge and expertise are critical for successful wine and fine spirits investing. Understanding the dynamics of the market, including trends, regional preferences, emerging producers, and changes in consumer tastes, can provide valuable insights for investment decisions. Engaging with the wine and spirits community, attending tastings, visiting vineyards or distilleries, and consulting experts or merchants can contribute to a deeper understanding of the market and potential investment opportunities.

Moreover, wine and fine spirits investments require a long-term perspective. Appreciation in value often occurs over an extended period, as the bottles age and become scarcer. Investors should be prepared to hold their investments for several years or even decades to realize the full potential returns.

Investors can employ various strategies in wine and fine spirits investing. One approach is to focus on wines or spirits from well-established regions or producers with a proven track record of value appreciation. Investing in prestigious Bordeaux wines, Burgundy wines, or rare Scotch whiskies, for example, can offer stability and a higher likelihood of consistent returns.

Another strategy is to explore emerging regions, new producers, or overlooked vintages that have the potential for value appreciation. These investment opportunities may offer unique growth prospects and the potential for discovering hidden gems.

Investors can also diversify their portfolios by investing in different wine regions, grape varietals, or spirit categories. Diversification spreads the risk and increases the likelihood of having successful investments that outweigh any potential losses.

Furthermore, wine and fine spirits investors can participate in auctions, wine funds, or private cellars. Auctions provide a platform to acquire rare and collectible bottles with transparent price discovery. Wine funds pool capital from multiple investors and invest in a diversified portfolio of wines. Private cellars allow investors to curate their collection and manage storage and acquisition directly.

In conclusion, investing in wine and fine spirits offers a unique combination of aesthetic pleasure, cultural value, and the potential for financial returns. With their inherent scarcity, historical significance, and increasing demand from collectors and connoisseurs, rare and collectible bottles have the potential to appreciate in value over time. Wine and fine spirits investments provide diversification benefits, as they have a low correlation with traditional financial assets. However, investing in these assets requires expertise in valuation, authentication, storage, and market trends. By conducting thorough research, engaging with the wine and spirits community, and adopting sound investment strategies, investors can navigate the complexities of wine and fine spirits investing and potentially reap the rewards of this captivating and rewarding alternative investment opportunity.

Allow me to offer a tip, contact Shoe Crazy Wine.

Shoe Crazy Wine is a wine company that was founded by Gwen Hurt, an entrepreneur and wine enthusiast. The brand aims to bring together two of Gwen Hurt's passions: shoes and wine. Based in the United States, Shoe Crazy Wine offers a variety of wines that are marketed with a unique and playful shoe theme.

Shoe Crazy Wine emphasizes the idea of celebrating life's moments and indulging in the pleasures it has to offer, just like a shoe lover cherishes the perfect pair of shoes. The brand aims to create a fun and memorable experience for wine enthusiasts, combining the joy of wine with the excitement of fashionable footwear.

The wine selection from Shoe Crazy Wine includes a range of red, white, and rosé wines. Each wine is crafted with a focus on quality, taste, and accessibility. The brand strives to offer wines that can be enjoyed by both casual wine drinkers and more discerning palates.

Shoe Crazy Wine also incorporates sustainability into its practices. The company is committed to using environmentally friendly packaging materials and reducing its carbon footprint.

In addition to producing wines, Shoe Crazy Wine is known for its philanthropic efforts. The company partners with various charitable organizations to support causes such as education, health, and empowerment.

As a relatively new wine brand, Shoe Crazy Wine has been gaining attention and recognition in the industry. Its unique concept and dedication to quality have garnered a growing fan base and positive reviews.

It's important to note that information about specific wine brands and their offerings may vary over time. For more information, go to their webpage: https://shoecrazywine.com. Or you can email them at customerservice@shoecrazywine.com. Be sure to tell them that "MR. LP." Steven Sykes sent you!

Royalty Financing:

Investing in Intellectual Property Royalties

Royalty financing is an alternative investment strategy that involves investing in the royalties generated from intellectual property assets such as music, books, patents, or trademarks. This form of investment allows investors to participate in the revenue streams generated by creative works or innovative ideas. By providing capital to intellectual property owners, investors can earn a share of the royalties as a return on their investment. This article will explore the concept of royalty financing, its types, benefits, risks, regulatory considerations, and factors that influence investment decisions.

Royalty financing involves providing capital to intellectual property owners in exchange for a share of the future royalties generated by their creative works or patented inventions. Intellectual property assets are intangible assets that include copyrights, trademarks, patents, or trade secrets. These assets can generate revenue through licensing agreements, sales, or other commercialization methods.

One of the primary forms of royalty financing is music royalties. Music artists, songwriters, and producers often enter into licensing agreements with record labels, music publishers, or streaming platforms to distribute and monetize their music. Royalty financing allows investors to provide upfront capital to musicians in exchange for a percentage of the royalties earned from their music sales, streaming, or public performances. This type of financing enables artists to access immediate funding while investors benefit from potential revenue generated by successful music catalogs.

Similarly, royalty financing can involve investing in royalties from books and literary works. Authors and publishers often receive royalties from book sales, ebook downloads, audiobook sales, or licensing deals. Investors can provide financing to authors or publishers in exchange for a share of the future royalty income. This form of financing can help authors with cash flow needs, support marketing efforts, or fund new book projects, while investors gain exposure to potential financial returns from successful literary works.

Another area of royalty financing is patent royalties. Patents provide inventors or businesses with exclusive rights to their inventions or innovations for a certain period. Royalty financing allows inventors or patent holders to monetize their patents by selling a portion of the future royalty income to investors. This type of financing can provide inventors with the necessary capital to further develop their inventions, fund research and development efforts, or expand their business operations, while investors participate in potential returns from successful patented technologies.

Royalty financing offers several benefits to investors. Firstly, it provides exposure to revenue streams generated by intellectual property assets without the need for direct involvement in their creation or commercialization. Investors can benefit from the creativity, innovation, and commercial success of others by sharing in the royalties generated by popular music, bestselling books, or patented technologies.

Moreover, royalty financing offers the potential for attractive risk-adjusted returns. Intellectual property assets with established track records of success or strong market demand can generate consistent royalty income over an extended period. By investing in proven or promising intellectual property, investors can access potential cash flows that are often stable and less susceptible to economic fluctuations compared to traditional investments.

Additionally, royalty financing can provide diversification benefits for investment portfolios. Royalty investments have a low correlation with traditional financial assets such as stocks or bonds. The performance of intellectual property royalties is influenced by factors specific to the creative or innovation industries, making them a distinct asset class. Including royalty investments can potentially enhance portfolio returns and reduce overall investment risk.

Furthermore, royalty financing allows investors to support creative endeavors, promote innovation, and contribute to the cultural landscape. By providing capital to artists, authors, inventors, or businesses, investors play a vital role in nurturing creativity and advancing technological advancements. Royalty financing can empower individuals or organizations to bring their ideas to fruition, create value, and make a lasting impact in their respective fields.

However, royalty financing also carries risks and considerations. The potential returns from royalty investments depend on the success and popularity of the intellectual property assets. Factors such as changing consumer preferences, competition, technological advancements, or legal and regulatory changes can impact the financial performance of intellectual property royalties. Investors need to conduct thorough due diligence, evaluate the quality and market potential of the intellectual property, and assess the reputation and track record of the creators or owners.

Moreover, royalty financing involves legal and contractual complexities. Investing in intellectual property royalties requires navigating licensing agreements, royalty structures, and ownership rights. Investors must ensure the proper documentation and legal protection of their investment, including rights to receive royalties and potential remedies in case of infringements or disputes. Seeking legal advice or partnering with experienced professionals can help mitigate legal risks associated with royalty financing.

Additionally, royalty investments can have long-term horizons and illiquid characteristics. The revenue generated by intellectual property assets often spans over several years or even decades. Investors should consider their investment horizon, liquidity needs, and risk tolerance when participating in royalty financing.

Regulatory considerations are also important in royalty financing. Intellectual property laws, licensing regulations, and copyright or patent protection mechanisms vary across jurisdictions. Investors should be aware of the legal and regulatory frameworks governing intellectual property rights in the countries where the assets are registered or commercialized. Compliance with intellectual property laws and regulations is crucial for protecting the investment and ensuring the legitimate collection of royalties.

In conclusion, royalty financing provides an alternative investment opportunity that allows investors to participate in the revenue streams generated by intellectual property assets. By providing capital to intellectual property owners, investors can earn a share of the royalties generated from music, books, patents, or other creative works. Royalty financing offers potential financial returns, diversification benefits, and the satisfaction of supporting creative endeavors and technological innovation. However, investing in royalty financing requires careful evaluation of intellectual property assets, legal considerations, and an understanding of market dynamics. Conducting thorough due diligence and seeking professional advice can help investors navigate the complexities of royalty financing and make informed investment decisions.

Peer-to-Peer Energy Trading:

Investing in Decentralized Energy Systems

Peer-to-peer (P2P) energy trading is a rapidly emerging form of alternative investing that leverages decentralized energy systems to enable individuals and businesses to trade excess energy directly with one another. This innovative approach to energy trading aims to create more sustainable and efficient energy markets while empowering individuals to actively participate in the energy transition. This article will explore the concept of peer-to-peer energy trading, its benefits, challenges, regulatory considerations, and the factors that influence investment decisions.

Peer-to-peer energy trading involves the direct exchange of energy between producers and consumers through a decentralized platform or technology. Traditionally, energy markets have been centralized, with large utility companies acting as intermediaries between energy producers and consumers. P2P energy trading disrupts this centralized model by enabling individuals and businesses to generate, store, and trade energy with one another in a peer-to-peer manner.

One of the key drivers of peer-to-peer energy trading is the proliferation of renewable energy sources such as solar and wind. Distributed energy generation, enabled by the widespread adoption of rooftop solar panels and small-scale wind turbines, allows individuals and businesses to generate their own electricity. P2P energy trading platforms leverage these decentralized energy sources by facilitating the direct exchange of excess energy between producers and consumers within a local or regional energy community.

P2P energy trading offers several benefits to participants. Firstly, it promotes energy self-sufficiency and resilience. Producers can generate their own energy, reducing reliance on centralized power grids and mitigating the risk of power outages. Consumers can access locally generated clean energy, supporting the transition to a more sustainable energy system.

Moreover, peer-to-peer energy trading provides a platform for individuals and businesses to monetize their excess energy. Producers can sell their surplus energy to consumers at a mutually agreed-upon price, creating additional revenue streams. Consumers, on the other hand, can access cheaper and greener energy by purchasing directly from local producers, bypassing the markups associated with traditional utility companies.

Additionally, peer-to-peer energy trading fosters community engagement and social interaction. Participants can engage in energy transactions with their neighbors or local businesses, strengthening community ties and promoting a sense of shared responsibility for sustainable energy consumption. P2P energy trading platforms often incorporate features that allow participants to track and monitor their energy usage, fostering a greater understanding of energy consumption patterns and promoting energy conservation practices.

Furthermore, P2P energy trading contributes to the decarbonization of the energy sector by facilitating the integration of renewable energy sources. By enabling the direct exchange of clean energy between producers and consumers, it encourages the adoption of distributed renewable energy generation. This decentralized approach reduces transmission losses and promotes energy efficiency, as energy is consumed closer to the point of generation.

However, peer-to-peer energy trading also faces challenges and considerations. One of the key challenges is the regulatory and legal framework. Energy markets are highly regulated, and the introduction of P2P energy trading disrupts the traditional roles of utilities and energy distributors. Regulatory frameworks need to adapt to accommodate P2P energy trading, ensuring the fair and secure operation of these decentralized systems while protecting the interests of all stakeholders.

Moreover, the scalability and technical challenges associated with P2P energy trading should be carefully addressed. As the number of participants and energy transactions increase, the technical infrastructure and grid management systems need to accommodate the additional complexities. Advanced metering, data management, and blockchain technologies are often utilized to ensure secure and transparent energy transactions in P2P energy trading platforms.

Additionally, risk management is a crucial consideration in P2P energy trading. Participants need to assess the risks associated with energy supply and demand fluctuations, price volatility, and the reliability of the energy infrastructure. Mitigating these risks often involves implementing mechanisms such as smart contracts, demand response programs, and energy storage systems to ensure a reliable and efficient energy trading process.

Furthermore, the financial viability of P2P energy trading should be carefully evaluated. The costs associated with implementing the necessary infrastructure, technology, and regulatory compliance can be significant. Investors and participants need to assess the potential return on investment and the business models associated with P2P energy trading platforms.

Investing in peer-to-peer energy trading can take different forms. Investors can participate by supporting the development and deployment of P2P energy trading platforms. This may involve investing in technology startups, software development companies, or renewable energy project developers that specialize in decentralized energy systems.

Another investment approach is to directly invest in renewable energy generation assets, such as solar panels or wind turbines, and participate in P2P energy trading as a producer. By generating excess energy and participating in local energy communities, investors can not only earn revenue from selling surplus energy but also contribute to the sustainability and resilience of the energy system.

Additionally, investors can participate as consumers in P2P energy trading platforms, purchasing locally generated clean energy from producers within their community. This allows investors to support the growth of renewable energy and reduce their carbon footprint while potentially benefiting from cost savings compared to traditional utility rates.

In conclusion, peer-to-peer energy trading offers a promising alternative investment opportunity that leverages decentralized energy systems to enable the direct exchange of energy between producers and consumers. P2P energy trading promotes energy self-sufficiency, resilience, community engagement, and the decarbonization of the energy sector. However, regulatory considerations, scalability challenges, risk management, and financial viability should be carefully evaluated. Investing in P2P energy trading can take different forms, including supporting the development of platforms, investing in renewable energy assets, or participating as consumers. As the energy transition continues to unfold, peer-to-peer energy trading presents an exciting avenue for investors to actively participate in the transformation of the energy system towards a more sustainable and decentralized future.

Timberland Investments:

Acquiring Forests for Sustainable Timber Production

Timberland investments are a form of alternative investing that involves acquiring forests or timberland with the objective of sustainable timber production. Investing in timberland provides individuals, institutions, and organizations with the opportunity to participate in the forest industry while potentially generating financial returns. This article will explore the concept of timberland investments, their benefits, risks, sustainability considerations, and the factors that influence investment decisions.

Timberland investments involve the acquisition and management of forests or timberland properties for timber production. Timber is a renewable resource, and sustainable timberland management practices ensure the long-term health and productivity of forests while providing a valuable raw material for various industries, such as construction, furniture, and paper.

One of the primary motivations for timberland investments is the potential for financial returns. Timberland properties can generate revenue through the sustainable harvest and sale of timber products. The value of timber is influenced by factors such as tree species, age, quality, market demand, and prevailing market prices. Over time, well-managed timberland has the potential to appreciate in value due to factors such as population growth, increased demand for wood products, and limited supply of forested land. Timberland investments can provide attractive risk-adjusted returns and diversification benefits to investment portfolios.

Moreover, investing in timberland contributes to environmental sustainability. Sustainable forest management practices promote the conservation of biodiversity, soil and water quality, and carbon sequestration. By investing in timberland, investors support the protection of forests, the preservation of ecosystems, and the mitigation of climate change. Timberland investments offer an opportunity to align financial goals with environmental stewardship and responsible land management.

Additionally, timberland investments offer a tangible asset with inherent value. Unlike many financial investments, timberland provides a physical presence and a connection to nature. Investors can appreciate the aesthetic beauty of forests, enjoy recreational activities such as hiking or hunting, and potentially benefit from non-timber forest products such as mushrooms or wild berries.

Furthermore, timberland investments can have positive social impacts. The forest industry often provides employment opportunities in rural communities, contributing to local economies and supporting livelihoods. Timberland management can promote sustainable development and community engagement through responsible forest practices, job creation, and the preservation of cultural heritage associated with forests.

However, timberland investments also carry risks and considerations. One of the primary risks is the volatility of timber prices. Timber prices can be influenced by factors such as supply and demand dynamics, changes in market conditions, and economic cycles. Investors need to carefully monitor market trends, engage in proactive forest management practices, and have a long-term investment horizon to mitigate the impact of price fluctuations.

Moreover, timberland investments require specialized knowledge and expertise. Successful timberland management involves understanding forest ecology, silvicultural practices, harvest planning, and timber marketing. Investors often partner with forestry professionals or forestry management companies to ensure effective forest operations, implement sustainable practices, and optimize financial returns.

Additionally, timberland investments require careful consideration of regulatory and legal frameworks. Forest management practices are subject to various environmental regulations, permitting requirements, and land use restrictions. Investors need to ensure compliance with applicable laws and regulations governing timber harvesting, forest certification, endangered species protection, and other environmental considerations.

Furthermore, timberland investments involve long investment horizons and illiquid characteristics. Forests typically have long growth cycles, requiring years or even decades for timber to reach maturity and be harvested. Investors should have a long-term investment horizon and be prepared for the illiquid nature of timberland assets. The exit strategy may involve selling the timberland property as a whole or in parcels to other investors, conservation organizations, or timber companies.

Sustainability considerations are paramount in timberland investments. Sustainable forest management practices focus on balancing economic, environmental, and social objectives. This includes responsible timber harvesting, reforestation efforts, biodiversity conservation, and protection of water resources. Investors committed to sustainability can seek certification from organizations such as the Forest Stewardship Council (FSC) or implement recognized sustainable forestry standards.

Timberland investments can take different forms. Direct ownership of timberland involves acquiring and managing forested properties independently. This approach requires significant capital, specialized knowledge, and active involvement in forest management. Investors have full control over decision-making processes and can implement their preferred forest management strategies.

Another approach is investing in timberland investment management organizations (TIMOs) or real estate investment trusts (REITs) specializing in timberland assets. TIMOs and timberland REITs pool investor capital to acquire and manage timberland properties on behalf of shareholders. Investing through TIMOs or REITs provides investors with the opportunity to access diversified timberland portfolios, professional management expertise, and potential liquidity through publicly traded REITs.

Furthermore, timberland investments can involve joint ventures or partnerships with existing landowners or forest product companies. These collaborations allow investors to leverage the knowledge and resources of established industry participants while sharing in the financial returns generated from sustainable timber production.

In conclusion, timberland investments offer an alternative investment opportunity that combines financial returns with environmental sustainability and social impact. Investing in timberland provides potential appreciation in value, diversification benefits, and a tangible asset connected to nature. However, careful consideration of market dynamics, regulatory frameworks, sustainability practices, and specialized knowledge is necessary to mitigate risks and optimize investment outcomes. Timberland investments can take different forms, including direct ownership, investing through TIMOs or timberland REITs, or forming joint ventures. By participating in timberland investments, individuals, institutions, and organizations can contribute to responsible forest management, biodiversity conservation, and the transition towards a more sustainable and resilient future.

Microfinance:

Empowering Individuals and Businesses in Developing Countries through Small Loans

Microfinance is a powerful tool in alternative investing that involves providing small loans and financial services to individuals and businesses in developing countries who have limited access to traditional banking services. This form of investment aims to alleviate poverty, promote entrepreneurship, and empower individuals to improve their livelihoods. By investing in microfinance, individuals and institutions can support economic development, social inclusion, and sustainable growth in underserved communities. This article will explore the concept of microfinance, its benefits, challenges, impact, and the factors that influence investment decisions.

Microfinance encompasses a range of financial services tailored to meet the needs of low-income individuals and micro-entrepreneurs, including small loans, savings accounts, insurance products, and financial literacy training. The primary focus of microfinance is to provide access to capital and financial services to individuals who are typically excluded from the formal banking sector due to lack of collateral, credit history, or proximity to banking infrastructure.

One of the key objectives of microfinance is poverty alleviation. By providing small loans to individuals and micro-businesses, microfinance institutions (MFIs) enable borrowers to invest in income-generating activities, such as starting or expanding a small business, purchasing productive assets, or investing in education or healthcare. These loans can serve as a catalyst for economic empowerment, allowing individuals to generate income, create employment opportunities, and improve their standard of living.

Moreover, microfinance promotes financial inclusion. In many developing countries, a significant portion of the population lacks access to basic financial services, such as savings accounts or insurance. Microfinance institutions fill this gap by providing tailored financial products and services that are accessible, affordable, and responsive to the specific needs of low-income individuals and micro-entrepreneurs. By extending financial services to the unbanked or underbanked populations, microfinance helps individuals build financial resilience, manage risks, and improve their financial well-being.

Additionally, microfinance fosters entrepreneurship and local economic development. Many individuals in developing countries possess the skills and entrepreneurial spirit to start and grow businesses but lack the necessary capital to do so. Microfinance bridges this financing gap by providing small loans to aspiring entrepreneurs, enabling them to invest in their businesses, purchase equipment or inventory, and expand their operations. By supporting local businesses and stimulating economic activity, microfinance contributes to job creation, poverty reduction, and the overall development of communities.

Furthermore, microfinance has a positive social impact, particularly on women and marginalized groups. In many societies, women face significant barriers to accessing financial services and economic opportunities. Microfinance addresses this gender gap by specifically targeting women borrowers, providing them with financial resources, training, and support to start and grow businesses. By empowering women financially, microfinance promotes gender equality, increases women's decision-making power, and improves social outcomes, including education, health, and overall well-being.

However, microfinance also faces challenges and considerations. One of the primary challenges is the risk associated with lending to individuals with limited credit history and collateral. MFIs must carefully assess the creditworthiness of borrowers and develop effective risk management systems to ensure loan repayment. This involves conducting thorough due diligence, implementing credit scoring models, adopting group lending approaches, and providing financial literacy training to borrowers.

Moreover, microfinance institutions need to strike a balance between social impact and financial sustainability. While the social mission of microfinance is paramount, MFIs also need to generate sufficient returns to cover their operational costs, loan loss provisions, and ensure the long-term viability of their operations. Achieving financial sustainability often requires finding the right balance between interest rates charged to borrowers, cost-effective delivery channels, effective risk management practices, and access to capital.

Additionally, regulatory frameworks and legal environments play a crucial role in microfinance. Regulatory regimes that are supportive, transparent, and proportionate are essential for the growth and stability of the microfinance sector. Effective regulation helps protect the interests of borrowers, ensures fair practices, promotes consumer confidence, and attracts investment in the industry. Investors in microfinance need to consider the regulatory landscape in the target country and assess the compliance and governance practices of the microfinance institutions they invest in.

Furthermore, impact measurement and social performance management are critical considerations in microfinance investments. Investors increasingly seek to measure the social impact of their investments and assess the effectiveness of microfinance institutions in achieving their social mission. Metrics such as the number of borrowers reached, poverty levels, women's empowerment indicators, and business growth rates are often used to evaluate the impact of microfinance. Investors should seek transparency and accountability from MFIs in reporting their social performance and measuring outcomes.

Microfinance investments can take different forms. Direct investments in microfinance institutions allow investors to provide capital to MFIs and participate in their loan portfolios. These investments often require due diligence on the financial and social performance of MFIs, as well as an understanding of the local context, regulatory framework, and risk management practices.

Another approach is investing in microfinance funds or vehicles. Microfinance funds pool investor capital and invest in a diversified portfolio of microfinance institutions or loans. These funds provide investors with access to a broader range of microfinance investments, professional management expertise, and potentially increased liquidity compared to direct investments.

Additionally, impact investing platforms and crowdfunding initiatives allow individual investors to support microfinance projects or specific borrowers directly. These platforms leverage technology and social networks to connect investors with microfinance opportunities, enabling them to contribute directly to the economic empowerment of individuals and communities.

In conclusion, microfinance is a powerful tool in alternative investing that empowers individuals and businesses in developing countries through small loans and financial services. It offers a pathway out of poverty, promotes financial inclusion, fosters entrepreneurship, and contributes to local economic development. By investing in microfinance, individuals and institutions can support sustainable and inclusive growth while generating potential financial returns. However, challenges such as credit risk management, financial sustainability, regulatory considerations, and impact measurement should be carefully evaluated. Microfinance investments can take various forms, including direct investments in microfinance institutions, investing in microfinance funds, or participating in impact investing platforms. By embracing microfinance, investors can play a pivotal role in promoting social and economic empowerment, creating positive change, and advancing the development agenda in underserved communities.

Litigation Finance:

Investing in Legal Claims for Potential Returns

Litigation finance, also known as litigation funding or legal financing, is an alternative investment strategy that involves investing in legal claims in exchange for a portion of the potential settlement or judgment. This form of investment provides capital to individuals or businesses involved in lawsuits, helping them cover legal expenses and alleviate financial burdens during the litigation process. Litigation finance offers investors the opportunity to diversify their portfolios and potentially earn attractive returns. This article will explore the concept of litigation finance, its benefits, risks, regulatory considerations, and factors that influence investment decisions.

Litigation finance involves providing capital to plaintiffs or law firms involved in ongoing legal disputes. The funds are used to cover legal fees, court costs, expert witness fees, and other litigation expenses. In return, the investor receives a portion of the potential settlement or judgment, typically structured as a predetermined percentage of the recovered amount.

One of the key benefits of litigation finance is its ability to level the playing field for plaintiffs with limited financial resources. Lawsuits can be costly and time-consuming, often putting significant financial strain on individuals or businesses seeking legal redress. Litigation finance provides access to capital that enables plaintiffs to pursue their claims without the need to bear the full financial burden. This promotes access to justice and allows individuals or businesses with meritorious claims to navigate the legal system on an equal footing.

Moreover, litigation finance offers a unique investment opportunity with the potential for attractive returns. By investing in legal claims, investors gain exposure to the potential upside of successful litigation outcomes. If the plaintiff prevails in the lawsuit or reaches a favorable settlement, the investor stands to benefit from a share of the financial recovery. This potential for significant returns makes litigation finance an appealing alternative investment for those seeking diversification and potentially high-risk-adjusted yields.

Additionally, litigation finance contributes to the efficiency of the legal system. By providing funding to plaintiffs, litigation finance helps reduce the burden on the courts and facilitates timely resolution of disputes. It allows individuals or businesses to pursue legitimate claims and ensures that the legal process is not unduly influenced by disparities in financial resources. Furthermore, litigation finance can incentivize settlement negotiations, as defendants may be more inclined to reach a favorable resolution when they face a well-funded plaintiff.

However, litigation finance is not without risks and considerations. One of the primary risks is the uncertainty inherent in litigation outcomes. Lawsuits can be unpredictable, and the final judgment or settlement may be lower than anticipated or even result in a loss. Investors need to carefully assess the merits of the legal claim, conduct thorough due diligence, and evaluate the potential risks and rewards before investing in litigation finance.

Moreover, the legal and regulatory landscape surrounding litigation finance varies across jurisdictions. Regulatory frameworks governing litigation finance may include restrictions, disclosure requirements, or ethical considerations. Investors need to be aware of the legal environment in the jurisdictions where they intend to invest and ensure compliance with applicable laws and regulations. Engaging legal counsel with expertise in litigation finance can help navigate these complexities and ensure adherence to legal and ethical standards.

Furthermore, potential conflicts of interest may arise in litigation finance arrangements. Investors need to carefully manage these conflicts to maintain the integrity and fairness of the litigation process. It is crucial to establish clear communication and transparency between the investor, the plaintiff, and their legal representation to avoid any perceived or actual impropriety.

Additionally, the timing of potential returns is an important consideration in litigation finance. Lawsuits can be protracted, and the duration of the litigation process may extend over several years. Investors should have a long-term investment horizon and be prepared for the illiquid nature of their investments. The exit strategy may involve waiting for the resolution of the lawsuit, reaching a settlement, or transferring the investment to another party.

Litigation finance investments can take different forms. Direct investments involve the investor directly funding a specific lawsuit in exchange for a share of the potential recovery. This approach requires thorough due diligence, legal expertise, and a deep understanding of the specific legal claim and associated risks.

Alternatively, investors can participate in litigation finance through specialized funds or platforms. Litigation finance funds pool investor capital and invest in a portfolio of legal claims, diversifying the investment across multiple lawsuits. This approach allows investors to spread their risk, gain access to a broader range of litigation opportunities, and benefit from professional fund management expertise.

In conclusion, litigation finance offers an alternative investment opportunity that provides capital to plaintiffs or law firms involved in legal disputes. It promotes access to justice, levels the playing field, and potentially generates attractive returns for investors. While litigation finance carries risks and considerations, including litigation uncertainty and regulatory complexities, careful due diligence and adherence to legal and ethical standards can mitigate these risks. Investors can participate in litigation finance through direct investments or by investing in specialized litigation finance funds. By embracing litigation finance, investors can contribute to the efficiency of the legal system, support legitimate claims, and potentially achieve compelling risk-adjusted returns in their investment portfolios.

Intellectual Property Investments:

Profiting from Patents, Trademarks, and Copyrights

Intellectual property (IP) investments are a form of alternative investing that involves acquiring and monetizing patents, trademarks, or copyrights for potential financial returns. Investing in IP allows individuals, businesses, and institutions to participate in the ownership and commercialization of innovative ideas, creative works, and brand assets. By acquiring and licensing IP rights, investors can generate revenue through licensing agreements, royalties, or the sale of IP assets. This article will explore the concept of IP investments, their benefits, challenges, strategies, and factors that influence investment decisions.

Intellectual property refers to intangible assets that are the result of human creativity or intellectual effort. It encompasses a broad range of forms, including inventions protected by patents, artistic works protected by copyrights, and brand assets protected by trademarks. IP investments involve acquiring ownership or licensing rights to these assets with the aim of generating financial returns.

One of the key benefits of IP investments is the potential for significant financial rewards. Successful patents, copyrighted works, or recognized trademarks can generate substantial revenue through licensing agreements. By owning or controlling valuable IP assets, investors can monetize their rights by granting licenses to third parties who wish to use the protected intellectual property. These licensing agreements often involve the payment of royalties, providing a stream of income for IP owners.

Moreover, IP investments offer diversification benefits to investment portfolios. Intellectual property assets have a unique risk-return profile that can be independent of traditional financial markets. The value of IP is based on its ability to generate revenue through commercialization, and its performance is influenced by factors such as market demand, innovation cycles, and legal protection. Including IP investments in a diversified portfolio can potentially enhance returns, reduce overall investment risk, and provide exposure to non-correlated assets.

Additionally, IP investments can foster innovation and support technological advancements. By investing in patents, investors contribute to the protection of inventions and the promotion of research and development. IP ownership provides inventors and businesses with the incentive to invest in innovative solutions and safeguards their competitive advantage. IP investments can drive economic growth, promote the transfer of knowledge, and create opportunities for collaboration between inventors and investors.

Furthermore, investing in IP allows for the strategic management of brand assets. Trademarks are valuable assets that represent the reputation, identity, and goodwill of a business or product. Investing in trademarks allows investors to acquire ownership or licensing rights to well-known brands, leveraging their market recognition and customer loyalty. Trademark licensing agreements can generate steady revenue streams and expand the reach of branded products or services.

However, IP investments also present challenges and considerations. One of the primary challenges is the complexity of assessing the value of IP assets. Determining the potential financial returns from patents, copyrights, or trademarks requires expertise in market analysis, licensing negotiations, and IP valuation methods. Investors need to carefully evaluate the market potential, competitive landscape, legal protection, and enforceability of the IP assets before making investment decisions.

Moreover, IP investments are subject to legal and regulatory considerations. Intellectual property rights vary across jurisdictions, and the legal landscape surrounding IP protection, enforcement, and licensing can be complex. Investors need to navigate intellectual property laws, patent offices, copyright registrations, and trademark systems to ensure the legitimate ownership and monetization of their IP assets. Engaging IP experts and legal professionals is crucial for assessing legal risks, conducting due diligence, and ensuring compliance with applicable laws and regulations.

Additionally, IP investments require active management and commercialization strategies. Simply owning IP assets does not guarantee financial success. Investors need to develop effective strategies for licensing, enforcing, or selling the IP rights. This may involve engaging licensing agents, partnering with IP management firms, or establishing in-house IP management capabilities. Successful IP commercialization requires understanding market dynamics, negotiating licensing agreements, monitoring infringement risks, and adapting to changing market conditions.

Furthermore, technological advancements and market disruptions can impact the value and relevance of IP assets. Emerging technologies, industry trends, and evolving consumer behaviors can render certain IP assets obsolete or less valuable over time. Investors need to stay abreast of technological advancements and market shifts to proactively manage their IP investments and identify opportunities for portfolio optimization.

IP investments can take different forms. Direct investments involve acquiring ownership rights to patents, copyrights, or trademarks. This approach requires conducting due diligence, negotiating licensing agreements, and managing the commercialization process independently. Direct investments offer greater control and potential for higher financial returns but require significant expertise and resources.

Alternatively, investors can participate in IP investments through specialized IP funds or investment platforms. IP funds pool investor capital and invest in a portfolio of IP assets, providing diversification and professional management expertise. Investing through IP funds allows investors to access a broader range of IP assets and leverage the fund's network and expertise in IP valuation, licensing, and enforcement.

Moreover, IP investments can involve partnerships or joint ventures with inventors, research institutions, or businesses. These collaborations allow investors to share the financial risks and rewards of IP ownership and commercialization. Joint ventures can provide access to innovative technologies, research pipelines, or established brand assets, enhancing the value and marketability of the IP investments.

In conclusion, IP investments offer a compelling alternative investment opportunity that allows investors to acquire, monetize, and profit from patents, trademarks, and copyrights. Investing in IP provides potential financial rewards, diversification benefits, and the opportunity to support innovation and brand management. However, IP investments require careful evaluation of the value, legal considerations, market dynamics, and commercialization strategies. Investors can participate in IP investments through direct ownership, investing in IP funds, or forming strategic partnerships. By embracing IP investments, individuals, businesses, and institutions can actively participate in the ownership and commercialization of valuable intellectual property assets and potentially benefit from their financial returns.

Cloud Real Estate:

Investing in the Future of Digital Infrastructure

Cloud real estate, also known as data center real estate or digital infrastructure, is an emerging form of alternative investing that focuses on acquiring and operating properties used for cloud computing, data storage, and other digital services. As the demand for cloud-based technologies and digital services continues to grow, investing in cloud real estate offers individuals, institutions, and businesses the opportunity to participate in the digital transformation and potentially generate attractive returns. This article will explore the concept of cloud real estate, its benefits, challenges, market trends, and factors that influence investment decisions.

Cloud real estate involves investing in properties that serve as the physical infrastructure for cloud computing and digital services. These properties typically include data centers, colocation facilities, and network infrastructure that support the storage, processing, and transmission of digital information. Cloud real estate investors own, lease, or operate these properties and provide essential infrastructure for technology companies, cloud service providers, and other organizations that rely on robust digital infrastructure.

One of the key benefits of investing in cloud real estate is the potential for long-term sustainable returns. The increasing reliance on cloud computing, big data, and digital services has created a growing demand for data centers and digital infrastructure. As more businesses and individuals shift their operations to the cloud, the need for secure, reliable, and scalable digital infrastructure continues to rise. Investing in cloud real estate allows investors to benefit from the ongoing demand for these critical facilities and potentially generate stable rental income or capital appreciation over time.

Moreover, cloud real estate investments offer diversification benefits to investment portfolios. The digital infrastructure sector has shown resilience and growth, even during economic downturns. Demand for cloud services and data storage remains strong regardless of market conditions, making cloud real estate investments attractive for diversifying portfolios and potentially reducing overall investment risk. As digital transformation continues across industries, investing in cloud real estate can provide exposure to a sector that is likely to experience long-term growth and stability.

Additionally, cloud real estate investments align with the increasing reliance on cloud-based technologies and digital services. As businesses and individuals adopt cloud computing, artificial intelligence, and other digital innovations, the need for robust digital infrastructure becomes critical. Investing in cloud real estate allows investors to participate in the expanding digital economy and support the growth of technology-driven businesses. By providing essential infrastructure, cloud real estate investors contribute to the development of a more connected and efficient digital ecosystem.

Furthermore, investing in cloud real estate presents an opportunity to contribute to sustainability and energy efficiency efforts. Data centers and digital infrastructure consume significant amounts of energy. However, advancements in technology and design have enabled more efficient and environmentally friendly data center operations. Investors in cloud real estate can play a role in supporting sustainable practices by investing in energy-efficient facilities, utilizing renewable energy sources, and promoting responsible resource management in data center operations.

However, cloud real estate investments also present challenges and considerations. One of the primary challenges is the technical expertise and knowledge required to evaluate and manage digital infrastructure assets. Understanding the intricacies of data center operations, network infrastructure, and evolving technologies is crucial for making informed investment decisions. Investors may need to partner with or engage technology experts, data center operators, or real estate professionals with domain expertise to navigate the complexities of the sector.

Moreover, cloud real estate investments require careful evaluation of market dynamics and location considerations. The demand for data center facilities can vary across regions, and selecting the right locations is essential to ensure proximity to major population centers, reliable power sources, connectivity options, and regulatory considerations. Investors need to assess the local market conditions, competitive landscape, and potential risks associated with specific geographical locations before making investment decisions.

Additionally, the technological advancements and evolving nature of cloud computing and digital services introduce risks related to obsolescence. As technology rapidly evolves, data center infrastructure needs to adapt and upgrade to meet changing demands. Investing in cloud real estate requires careful consideration of the quality of the facility, scalability options, and the ability to accommodate future technological advancements. Staying abreast of emerging technologies and industry trends is essential for ensuring the long-term viability and competitiveness of cloud real estate investments.

Furthermore, cloud real estate investments may involve partnerships or joint ventures with technology companies, data center operators, or real estate developers. Collaborations allow investors to leverage the expertise and resources of industry participants while sharing the financial risks and rewards associated with digital infrastructure investments. These partnerships can provide access to specialized knowledge, networks, and operational efficiencies in managing and operating cloud real estate assets.

Cloud real estate presents an emerging opportunity for alternative investing that aligns with the increasing reliance on cloud-based technologies and digital services. Investing in cloud real estate offers potential long-term sustainable returns, diversification benefits, and participation in the digital transformation. However, careful evaluation of market dynamics, technical expertise, location considerations, and technological advancements is necessary. Cloud real estate investments can take various forms, including direct ownership, partnerships, or joint ventures with technology companies or data center operators. By investing in cloud real estate, individuals, institutions, and businesses can support the growth of the digital economy, contribute to sustainability efforts, and potentially benefit from the ongoing demand for robust digital infrastructure.

There are several cloud real estate platforms that provide access to investment opportunities in the digital infrastructure sector. Here are some notable platforms:

1. DigitalBridge: DigitalBridge is a cloud real estate investment platform that focuses on providing access to digital infrastructure assets, including data centers and cell towers. The platform allows accredited investors to invest in institutional-quality digital infrastructure projects through a user-friendly online platform.

2. CrowdStreet: CrowdStreet is a crowdfunding platform that offers a range of real estate investment opportunities, including cloud real estate. The platform connects investors with vetted commercial real estate projects, including data centers and other technology-related properties. Investors can browse investment offerings, review project details, and make investment decisions online.

3. Equinix Marketplace: Equinix is a global data center and colocation provider. Through their Equinix Marketplace platform, investors can explore investment opportunities in Equinix data centers. The platform provides information on available data center assets, leasing options, and potential investment returns.

4. EdgeConneX Marketplace: EdgeConneX is a data center operator specializing in edge computing solutions. Their EdgeConneX Marketplace allows investors to explore investment opportunities in edge data centers and related infrastructure. The platform provides information on available projects, market insights, and investment resources.

5. Aligned: Aligned is a data center infrastructure company that offers sustainable and scalable data center solutions. Their platform provides information on their data center portfolio, investment opportunities, and sustainable design features. Accredited investors can explore potential investments in Aligned's data center projects.

6. DC BLOX: DC BLOX is a data center provider that focuses on underserved markets in the Southeastern United States. Their platform offers information on their data center locations, services, and investment opportunities. Investors can explore potential investments in DC BLOX data centers through their platform.

When considering any cloud real estate platform, it's essential to conduct thorough due diligence on the platform's reputation, track record, and compliance with regulatory requirements. Additionally, investors should carefully review investment offerings, investment terms, and associated risks before making investment decisions. Engaging with financial advisors or legal professionals who specialize in real estate or alternative investments can provide guidance and assistance in navigating the platform and investment process.

Crowdfunding Real Estate:

Revolutionizing Access to Real Estate Investments

Crowdfunding real estate has emerged as a game-changing approach to alternative investing, revolutionizing the way individuals and institutions participate in real estate projects. This innovative model allows investors to pool their funds through online platforms and invest in a diverse range of real estate opportunities, including residential, commercial, and mixed-use properties. Crowdfunding real estate offers numerous benefits, such as increased accessibility, diversification, transparency, and the potential for attractive returns. This article will delve into the concept of crowdfunding real estate, its advantages, challenges, regulatory considerations, and factors that influence investment decisions.

Crowdfunding real estate involves the collective investment of funds from a large number of individuals or institutions into real estate projects through online platforms. These platforms, known as real estate crowdfunding platforms or real estate investment platforms, facilitate the process by connecting investors with real estate developers, operators, or sponsors seeking capital for their projects. Investors can browse through a variety of investment opportunities, review project details, and choose to invest in properties that align with their investment objectives and risk tolerance.

One of the key benefits of crowdfunding real estate is its ability to democratize access to real estate investments. Historically, real estate investing was often limited to high-net-worth individuals or institutions due to high entry barriers, such as substantial capital requirements, extensive networks, and specialized knowledge. Crowdfunding real estate opens up investment opportunities to a broader range of investors, allowing individuals to invest with smaller amounts of capital and gain exposure to real estate assets that were previously inaccessible.

Moreover, crowdfunding real estate offers diversification benefits to investment portfolios. By investing in multiple real estate projects across different locations, property types, and risk profiles, investors can spread their risk and potentially enhance their risk-adjusted returns. Real estate crowdfunding platforms provide a curated selection of investment opportunities, enabling investors to build a diversified real estate portfolio without the need for extensive market research or direct property management.

Additionally, crowdfunding real estate provides increased transparency and visibility into investment opportunities. Real estate crowdfunding platforms typically provide detailed project information, financial projections, risk assessments, and other relevant data to help investors make informed investment decisions. This transparency allows investors to assess the merits of each opportunity, evaluate the track record of the project sponsors, and understand the potential risks and rewards associated with the investment.

Furthermore, crowdfunding real estate offers various investment structures, allowing investors to choose the investment approach that suits their preferences. Common investment structures include equity investments, where investors become partial owners of the property and participate in potential rental income and appreciation, and debt investments, where investors provide loans to developers or sponsors in exchange for regular interest payments. Investors can select the investment structure that aligns with their risk appetite, investment horizon, and desired level of involvement in the project.

However, crowdfunding real estate also presents challenges and considerations. One challenge is the potential lack of liquidity compared to traditional investment vehicles. Real estate investments are typically long-term commitments, and early exits may be limited or subject to certain restrictions. Investors should have a clear understanding of the investment timeline and be prepared to hold their investment until the project reaches maturity or an exit opportunity arises.

Moreover, investors need to carefully evaluate the credibility and track record of the project sponsors or developers when considering crowdfunding real estate investments. Thorough due diligence on the sponsor's experience, past performance, financial stability, and adherence to regulatory requirements is crucial to assess the viability and credibility of the investment opportunity. Engaging with professionals, such as real estate attorneys or financial advisors, can provide valuable guidance in evaluating investment offerings and conducting due diligence.

Additionally, regulatory considerations play a significant role in crowdfunding real estate. Regulatory frameworks surrounding crowdfunding vary across jurisdictions, and platforms must comply with applicable securities laws, investor protection regulations, and reporting requirements. Investors should familiarize themselves with the regulatory landscape in their jurisdiction and choose platforms that operate in compliance with applicable regulations to ensure investor protection and transparency.

Furthermore, market conditions and economic factors can influence the performance of crowdfunding real estate investments. Real estate markets are subject to fluctuations, and factors such as supply and demand dynamics, interest rates, and local economic conditions can impact property values and rental income. Investors should consider the macroeconomic environment, market trends, and the specific risks associated with each investment opportunity to make informed investment decisions.

Crowdfunding real estate investments can take different forms. Some platforms offer direct investments, allowing investors to participate directly in specific real estate projects. Other platforms operate as real estate investment trusts (REITs), where investors can purchase shares in a diversified portfolio of real estate assets. Each approach has its own advantages and considerations, and investors should choose the investment structure that aligns with their investment goals and preferences.

In conclusion, crowdfunding real estate has revolutionized the accessibility and dynamics of real estate investing. It offers individuals and institutions the opportunity to diversify their portfolios, gain exposure to real estate assets, and participate in investment opportunities that were once reserved for a select few. While crowdfunding real estate provides numerous benefits, careful evaluation of investment offerings, regulatory compliance, and due diligence on project sponsors are essential. Investors should choose reputable platforms, conduct thorough research, and consider professional advice to navigate the crowdfunding real estate landscape successfully. By embracing crowdfunding real estate, investors can unlock the potential of real estate investing and potentially achieve attractive risk-adjusted returns.

Alternative Investing Platform Suggestions:

1. AngelList: AngelList is a leading platform for early-stage investing, connecting startups with accredited investors. It offers opportunities to invest in a wide range of startups across industries. [Website: https://angel.co/]

2. CircleUp: CircleUp focuses on consumer brands and offers accredited investors access to investment opportunities in innovative consumer product companies. [Website: https://circleup.com/]

3. SeedInvest: SeedInvest is an equity crowdfunding platform that provides access to a curated selection of startup investment opportunities. It offers opportunities for both accredited and non-accredited investors. [Website: https://www.seedinvest.com/]

4. RealtyMogul: RealtyMogul is a real estate crowdfunding platform that allows investors to invest in a range of commercial properties, including office buildings, apartments, and retail spaces. [Website: https://www.realtymogul.com/]

5. Fundrise: Fundrise is a real estate investment platform that offers individuals the ability to invest in a diversified portfolio of commercial real estate assets. It provides access to both debt and equity investments. [Website: https://fundrise.com/]

6. PeerStreet: PeerStreet is a peer-to-peer lending platform that allows accredited investors to invest in real estate-backed loans. It offers opportunities to participate in various residential and commercial real estate projects. [Website: https://www.peerstreet.com/]

7. LendingClub: LendingClub is a peer-to-peer lending platform that connects borrowers with individual and institutional investors. It provides opportunities to invest in personal loans. [Website: https://www.lendingclub.com/]

8. Wefunder: Wefunder is an equity crowdfunding platform that enables investors to support early-stage companies and startups. It offers investment opportunities across industries. [Website: https://wefunder.com/]

9. Groundfloor: Groundfloor is a real estate lending platform that allows investors to participate in short-term real estate loans. It provides opportunities for both accredited and non-accredited investors. [Website: https://www.groundfloor.com/]

10. YieldStreet: YieldStreet is an alternative investment platform that offers access to a range of asset-backed investment opportunities, including real estate, art, and legal finance. [Website: https://www.yieldstreet.com/]

11. Patch of Land: Patch of Land is a peer-to-peer lending platform that specializes in short-term real estate loans. It provides opportunities to invest in residential and commercial real estate projects. [Website: https://patchofland.com/]

12. Artivest: Artivest is an investment platform that focuses on alternative investments, including private equity, hedge funds, and real estate. It provides access to institutional-quality investment opportunities. [Website: https://www.artivest.co/]

13. Cadre: Cadre is a platform that offers access to institutional-grade real estate investments. It provides opportunities to invest in commercial properties across various asset classes. [Website: https://www.cadre.com/]

14. EquityMultiple: EquityMultiple is a real estate crowdfunding platform that allows investors to participate in commercial real estate projects. It offers opportunities to invest in properties with institutional-grade sponsors. [Website: https://www.equitymultiple.com/]

15. AlphaFlow: AlphaFlow is an investment platform that provides access to real estate-backed loans and portfolios. It allows investors to diversify their real estate investments across multiple loans. [Website: https://www.alphaflow.com/]

16. Republic: Republic is an equity crowdfunding platform that offers investment opportunities in startups, real estate, video games, and more. It provides access to both accredited and non-accredited investors. [Website: https://republic.co/]

17. Circle Yield: Circle Yield is a platform that offers access to yield-generating alternative investments, including digital assets and crypto-based opportunities. [Website: https://www.circleyield.com/]

18. CrowdStreet: CrowdStreet is a real estate investment platform that connects accredited investors with institutional-quality commercial real estate projects. It provides opportunities to invest in a range of property types and locations. [Website: https://www.crowdstreet.com/]

19. YieldX: YieldX is an investment platform that offers access to alternative investments, including private equity, real estate, and venture capital. It provides opportunities to diversify investment portfolios. [Website: https://yieldx.com/]

20. Prodigy Network: Prodigy Network is a real estate crowdfunding platform that focuses on commercial real estate investments. It offers opportunities to invest in office buildings, hotels, and mixed-use projects. [Website: https://www.prodigynetwork.com/]

21. YieldX Prime: YieldX Prime is an investment platform that offers access to a wide range of alternative investments, including private equity, real estate, and venture capital. It provides investors with opportunities to diversify their portfolios and potentially achieve attractive returns. [Website: https://yieldxprime.com/]

22. Small Change: Small Change is a real estate crowdfunding platform that focuses on impact investing. It offers opportunities to invest in real estate projects that promote social and environmental benefits, such as affordable housing and sustainable development. [Website: https://www.smallchange.com/]

23. Cadence: Cadence is an investment platform that offers fractional investments in alternative assets. It provides access to a range of

investment opportunities, including private credit, structured notes, and other fixed-income products. [Website: https://withcadence.io/]

24. Harvest Returns: Harvest Returns is an agricultural crowdfunding platform that allows investors to participate in agriculture and farming projects. It provides opportunities to invest in farmland, timberland, livestock, and other agricultural ventures. [Website: https://www.harvestreturns.com/]

25. RealtyShares: RealtyShares is a real estate crowdfunding platform that provides access to a variety of commercial real estate projects. It offers opportunities to invest in properties such as office buildings, multi-family residences, and industrial facilities. [Website: N/A - RealtyShares has ceased operations]

26. Angel Invest Boston: Angel Invest Boston is an angel investing platform that connects accredited investors with promising early-stage companies. It focuses on investing in startups in the Greater Boston area and provides resources and networking opportunities for investors. [Website: https://www.angelinvestboston.com/]

27. Patch Homes: Patch Homes is an alternative home financing platform that offers homeowners the opportunity to access home equity without taking on additional debt. It allows homeowners to receive a cash advance in exchange for a share of the future appreciation of their home. [Website: https://www.patchhomes.com/]

28. Groundbreaker: Groundbreaker is a real estate investment software platform that helps real estate syndicators, fund managers, and developers streamline their investment processes. It provides tools for

investor management, fundraising, and reporting. [Website: https://www.groundbreaker.co/]

29. StartEngine: StartEngine is an equity crowdfunding platform that allows both accredited and non-accredited investors to invest in a wide range of startups and growth companies. It offers opportunities to support innovative businesses across various industries. [Website: https://www.startengine.com/]

30. Cadre: Cadre is a real estate investment platform that provides access to institutional-grade commercial real estate opportunities. It offers opportunities to invest in properties such as office buildings, hotels, and multi-family residences. [Website: https://www.cadre.com/]

31. Republic Real Estate: Republic Real Estate is a crowdfunding platform that offers investment opportunities in real estate projects. It allows both accredited and non-accredited investors to invest in residential, commercial, and mixed-use properties. [Website: https://republic.co/real-estate]

32. Roofstock: Roofstock is an online marketplace for single-family rental properties. It allows investors to buy, sell, and manage investment properties remotely, providing an accessible and efficient way to invest in the rental property market. [Website: https://www.roofstock.com/]

33. The RealReal: The RealReal is an online luxury consignment marketplace that offers investors the opportunity to participate in the resale of luxury fashion and accessories. It provides a platform for

individuals to buy and sell authenticated luxury items. [Website: https://www.therealreal.com/]

34. Fundable: Fundable is an equity crowdfunding platform that connects startups and early-stage companies with accredited investors. It provides opportunities for investors to support innovative businesses and potentially participate in their growth. [Website: https://www.fundable.com/]

35. FarmTogether: FarmTogether is an agricultural investment platform that enables investors to own fractional shares of farmland. It offers opportunities to invest in US farmland, providing exposure to the agricultural sector and potential long-term returns. [Website: https://farmtogether.com/]

36. Circle Yield: Circle Yield is a digital asset investment platform that offers access to yield-generating opportunities in the crypto and decentralized finance (DeFi) space. It allows investors to participate in lending, staking, and liquidity mining activities. [Website: https://www.circleyield.com/]

37. OpenInvest: OpenInvest is an impact investing platform that allows investors to build customized portfolios aligned with their values. It offers opportunities to invest in companies that promote social and environmental impact while aiming to deliver financial returns. [Website: https://www.openinvest.co/]

38. M1 Finance: M1 Finance is a digital investment platform that combines automated investing with customization. It offers users the ability to create personalized investment portfolios, known as "pies,"

that can include stocks, ETFs, and other assets. M1 Finance also provides features like automatic rebalancing and fractional share investing. [Website: https://www.m1finance.com/]

39. Rally Rd: Rally Rd is an alternative investing platform that allows individuals to invest in shares of rare collectibles, classic cars, and other high-value assets. It enables users to own fractional shares of these assets, making it more accessible to a wider range of investors. Rally Rd also provides information and insights about the assets to help investors make informed decisions. [Website: https://www.rallyrd.com/]

40. Prosper: Prosper is a peer-to-peer lending platform that connects borrowers with individual and institutional investors. It offers personal loans for a variety of purposes, such as debt consolidation, home improvement, and small business financing. Investors can fund these loans and potentially earn returns based on the interest paid by borrowers. [Website: https://www.prosper.com/]

41. Modiv: Modiv is an online real estate investment platform that focuses on commercial real estate opportunities. It allows accredited investors to invest in pre-vetted, income-producing properties through real estate investment trusts (REITs) or direct ownership. Modiv aims to provide access to institutional-quality real estate investments with low minimum investment requirements. [Website: https://www.modiv.com/]

42. Flippa: Flippa is an online marketplace for buying and selling online businesses, websites, and domain names. It connects buyers and

sellers looking to engage in transactions related to digital assets. Flippa provides a platform for listing and discovering a wide range of online businesses and digital properties. [Website: https://www.flippa.com/]

43. Mynd: Mynd is a property management platform that uses technology and data-driven insights to streamline property management processes. It offers services such as tenant screening, rent collection, and maintenance coordination for residential properties. Mynd aims to provide property owners with a more efficient and hassle-free property management experience. [Website: https://www.mynd.co/]

44. Realty Mogul: Realty Mogul is a real estate crowdfunding platform that allows investors to access a variety of commercial real estate investment opportunities. It offers both debt and equity investments in properties such as office buildings, retail spaces, and multi-family residences. Realty Mogul aims to make real estate investing more accessible and efficient. [Website: https://www.realtymogul.com/]

45. EquityNet: EquityNet is an equity crowdfunding platform that connects entrepreneurs seeking capital with investors. It provides a platform for companies to showcase their investment opportunities and raise funds from accredited investors. EquityNet aims to simplify the fundraising process and facilitate connections between entrepreneurs and investors. [Website: https://www.equitynet.com/]

46. Diversity Fund: Diversity Fund is an online investment platform that focuses on providing investment opportunities in digital assets,

including cryptocurrencies and other alternative investments. It allows individuals to invest in a diversified portfolio of digital assets and aims to generate returns in the emerging digital economy. [Website: https://www.diversity.fund/]

REFERENCES

1. Swensen, D. F. (2009). Pioneering Portfolio Management: An Unconventional Approach to Institutional Investment. Free Press.

2. Lerner, J., & Tufano, P. (Eds.). (2011). The Venture Capital Cycle (2nd ed.). MIT Press.

3. Jones, D. T. (2012). Angel Investing: The Gust Guide to Making Money and Having Fun Investing in Startups. Wiley.

4. Ritter, J. R., & Welch, I. (Eds.). (2016). The Research Handbook of IPOs. Edward Elgar Publishing.

5. D'Arcy, D. (2013). Hedge Fund Investing: A Practical Approach to Understanding Investor Motivation, Manager Profits, and Fund Performance. Wiley.

6. Kochis, J. J., & West, S. J. (2012). The New Advisor for Life: Become the Indispensable Financial Advisor to Affluent Families. Wiley.

7. Roulac, S. (2013). Real Estate GameChangers: The Extraordinary People and Strategies that Transformed the Real Estate Industry. Wiley.

8. Lonsdale, J., & Lonsdale, M. (2016). The Entrepreneur's Guide to Equity Crowdfunding: A Systematic Guide to Using the JOBS Act to Raise Funds. Wiley.

9. Douthett, E. B., & Kunsch, P. L. (2018). Fundamentals of Financial Planning. CFP Board.

10. Broughton, J. (2013). The Eurobond Market: The Internationalization of the Eurocurrency Market (2nd ed.). Palgrave Macmillan.

11. Fink, M. L. (2013). A Legal Guide to Urban and Sustainable Development for Planners, Developers and Architects. Wiley.

12. Lerner, J., & Hardymon, G. F. (Eds.). (2012). Venture Capital and Private Equity: A Casebook (5th ed.). Wiley.

13. Paglia, J., & Shailer, G. (2012). Real Estate and Globalisation. Wiley.

14. Koller, T., Dobbs, R., Huyett, B., & Palter, R. (2015). Value: The Four Cornerstones of Corporate Finance. Wiley.

15. Bodie, Z., Kane, A., & Marcus, A. J. (2014). Investments (10th ed.). McGraw-Hill Education.

16. Damodaran, A. (2012). Investment Valuation: Tools and Techniques for Determining the Value of Any Asset (3rd ed.). Wiley.

17. Kiyosaki, R. T., & Lechter, S. L. (2017). Rich Dad's Guide to Investing: What the Rich Invest In That the Poor and Middle Class Do Not! Plata Publishing.

18. Fabozzi, F. J., & Markowitz, H. M. (Eds.). (2002). The Theory and Practice of Investment Management: Asset Allocation, Valuation, Portfolio Construction, and Strategies (2nd ed.). Wiley.

19. Feld, B., & Mendelson, J. (2016). Venture Deals: Be Smarter than Your Lawyer and Venture Capitalist. Wiley.

20. Preqin Ltd. (2021). Preqin Global Alternatives Reports. Retrieved from https://www.preqin.com/insights/reports

21. Moreira, A., & Muir, T. (2017). Volatility Managed Portfolios. Journal of Financial Economics, 124(1), 1-23.

22. EY. (2020). Global Private Equity Divestment Study. Retrieved from https://www.ey.com/en_gl/transactions/private-equity/global-private-equity-divestment-study

23. Daskalaki, C., & Skiadopoulos, G. (2011). Should Investors Include Commodities in their Portfolios After All? New Evidence. Journal of Banking & Finance, 35(10), 2606-2626.

24. Khandani, A. E., & Lo, A. W. (2011). What Happened to the Quants in August 2007? Journal of Investment Management, 9(2), 1-14.

25. Lerner, J., & Schoar, A. (Eds.). (2019). Venture Capital: A Global Perspective. Cambridge University Press.

26. Henderson, B. J., & Pearson, N. D. (2011). Investing with Hedge Funds: Examining the Benefits and Risks. Financial Analysts Journal, 67(1), 60-80.

27. Eckbo, B. E. (Ed.). (2016). Handbook of Corporate Finance: Empirical Corporate Finance (Vol. 2). Elsevier.

28. Chakrabarty, B., & Roll, R. (2002). East Asia and Europe During the 1997 Asian Collapse: A Clinical Study of a Financial Crisis. Journal of Financial Markets, 5(1), 1-30.

29. Harris, R., & Gurel, E. (1986). Price and Volume Effects Associated with Changes in the S&P 500 List: New Evidence for the Existence of Price Pressures. Journal of Finance, 41(4), 815-829.

30. Chesbrough, H. (2006). Open Innovation: The New Imperative for Creating and Profiting from Technology. Harvard Business Press.

31. Khanna, T., & Palepu, K. (2010). Winning in Emerging Markets: A Road Map for Strategy and Execution. Harvard Business Press.

32. Brown, G. W., & Goetzmann, W. N. (1995). Performance Persistence. Journal of Finance, 50(2), 679-698.

33. Bienz, C., & Walz, U. (2007). Evolution of Decision and Control Rights in Venture Capital Contracts: An Empirical Analysis. Journal of Financial Intermediation, 16(3), 368-399.

34. Lummer, S. L., & McConnell, J. J. (1989). Further Evidence on the Bank Lending Process and the Capital-Market Response to Bank Loan Agreements. Journal of Financial Economics, 25(1), 99-122.

35. Merton, R. C. (1990). Continuous-Time Finance. Blackwell Publishers.

Epilogue:

A Journey of Empowerment and Change

As Unity 1 of The Wealth Faction Financial Series: The Viability of Alternative Investing ends, I, Steven L. Sykes, fondly known as "MR. LP," reflect upon this incredible journey with a heart brimming with joy, a sense of fulfillment, and immense pride. It has been a labor of love to share this valuable information with the broader community, including communities of color. The ability to provide verified research and insights into alternative investing has been both an honor and a responsibility—one that I gladly embraced.

In the world of finance, access to reliable information can be a game-changer, and The Wealth Faction Series was designed with the intent of making this knowledge accessible to all. Empowering individuals with the understanding of alternative investing has the potential to transform lives and secure a brighter future for generations to come. We firmly believe that knowledge is the catalyst for change and progress, and by equipping people with the right tools, we enable them to build a better financial future.

We understand that everyone's financial journey is unique, and alternative investing might not be suitable for everyone. However, we encourage everyone to take the time to explore and make informed decisions, no matter how small. Even a single change can have a profound impact, not only on one's life but also on the lives of their loved ones and future generations.

Throughout this series, we have witnessed the positive impact it has had on countless individuals, and the support and feedback from our readers have been a constant source of inspiration. We thank each one of you for joining us on this enlightening journey, and we remain committed to supporting you in your financial endeavors.

As we turn our attention to our next book, Unity 2 of The Wealth Faction Series, titled "The Financial Suffering BIPOC Suffered," we recognize the significance of addressing financial horrors that have affected communities of color, not just on a financial level but also psychologically, emotionally, and physically. Shedding light on these issues is vital to create a more inclusive and equitable financial landscape.

In closing, we extend our gratitude to all those who have contributed to this series and embraced our mission of spreading financial literacy. To all readers, we encourage you to continue exploring and learning. Should you have any questions, comments, or concerns, please do not hesitate to reach out to me via email at thewealthfaction@gmail.com.

May the knowledge gained from The Wealth Faction Financial Series serve as a catalyst for positive change in your lives and the lives of those around you. May we all strive to create a better and more prosperous future for ourselves and our communities. God bless you all.

With sincere appreciation and warm regards,

Steven L. Sykes (MR. LP)

Made in United States
Orlando, FL
09 November 2023

38744214R00072